The Wounded Leader

Deliverance And Healing From The Aftermath of Trauma

Kimberly Moses

REJOICE
Essential Publishing

ISBN-13: 978-1-956775-79-2

Foreword

Kimberly Moses is a prophet. As such, she has gone through so much in her life and has the battle scars to prove it. If you're a prophet, then you have an idea of the warfare that goes along with the gift. Though Moses was challenged by the enemy, the transformation that manifested in her life is wholly supernatural. Kimberly has experienced the trauma that comes from being abused by leaders and everyday people in her life whom she trusted. Though there has been tremendous hurt in her past, she went through it all for our benefit. As a wounded leader herself, Kim has an obligation to those who are suffering in silence. I believe she's authorized by God to heal, encourage, and deliver those that clergy have abused and vice versa. Moses wants to lighten the burden of leaders and laypersons who are carrying the weights of guilt, shame, and discouragement. The Lord has mended her spiritual injuries and bandaged her emotional wounds. Now, through her ministry and this book that you are reading, she wants you to enjoy that same freedom.

"God heals the brokenhearted and binds up their wounds." —*Psalm 147:3*

In her latest book, *The Wounded Leader*, Kimberly Moses uses a myriad of very personal stories to teach major life lessons. Here, she generously uses

Scripture throughout this literary work to give more weight to her words. Kimberly Moses explains the consequences of holding onto the offense that may come as a consequence of being hurt by someone. She is so transparent in her writing. Kimberly opens up regarding very personal encounters. Throughout this book, you can literally hear her heart! She has such a burden for "wounded soldiers," and it shows on just about every page. Moses provides prayers and declarations that you can use to assist in getting healed from the things that hurt you. She also addresses the various dangers that may have been birthed out of woundedness and provides solutions to them. This work was birthed out of years of the pain that accompanies authentic ministry.

As I read her manuscript, I was amazed that she tackled some very tough subject matters such as pride, competition, dishonor, division, loneliness, etc. These are issues that many of us go through often. I believe that God has a specific assignment for many of His Leaders today. He has called them to heal the brokenhearted and bind up their wounds. I think that this is exactly what Moses' book will do for those that read it. Her various real-world experiences are likely to resonate with much that you've gone through, whether you lead a church or a household. Many of the five-fold will see themselves in Moses' accounts. If you're a wounded leader, then this is just the book to help you to heal.

Dr. John Veal
Author of the books
Supernaturally Prophetic
Supernaturally Delivered
Racism: The Church and the Nation (Coauthor)

Acknowledgments

I had to go through some very trying times to write this manuscript. Writing this took me over a year because I needed to heal and not write from a wounded place. I often stopped typing and cried out to God to strengthen me to continue. If you are one of the people who hurt me and happen to read this, I love you, and my heart is not to bash you. What happened between us was something that I had to experience to get to my next level. It's my story and a part of my journey to be able to minister to leaders more effectively. Nothing in God is wasted. He used my pain for His glory.

Table of Contents

Introduction

Many people do not realize the pain that some leaders carry. So much pressure is placed upon them that they are afraid to be seen as weak or vulnerable, so they hold in their feelings. Not everyone can handle a leader's humanity because they have been placed on a pedestal. If a leader has a moment of weakness, their name is slandered on social media, and people question their ability to lead. People don't realize that leaders are flesh just like them. They bleed, get sick, and have emotions.

It's shocking to see many pastors commit suicide, renouncing their faith, and leaving the ministry. We don't know the intensity of the pain they may have been battling internally. Throughout scripture, various leaders are hurt by those they were leading. David's son Absalom turned against him and tried to take his kingdom (2 Samuel 15-19). Imagine how David must've felt. The devil is using your own flesh and blood to destroy you and your legacy. Your son, who you love dearly, wants to see your demise. That level of betrayal is excruciating. Yet David still had to lead because he was a mighty warrior and King with many followers.

Moses and Aaron, two prophets leading the Israelites to the Promised Land, were attacked many times by those they were leading. The sons of Korah thought they could do a better job than Moses and Aaron, and these men turned people against them (Numbers 16). Think about being in Moses' and Aaron's shoes. It hurts when you find out "brother and sister so and so" said such awful things about you and their real thoughts concerning you. The true intentions of their heart have now become exposed, but you still have to love them. When the attack on Moses and Aaron occurred, they fell to the ground and worshipped the Lord. The Lord eventually opened up the earth and swallowed the sons of Korah. As Moses and Aaron worshipped the Lord during a mob attack, you also have to. In the natural, thousands of men were against them, so it seemed like they were outnumbered. We must remember that there are more fighting for us than against us (2 Kings 6:16).

A leader such as a pastor, evangelist, apostle, prophet, or those on the front line in ministry have a greater target on their backs from the enemy. When God uses them extensively in healing and deliverance, this angers the enemy, causing retaliatory attacks. The same spirits that they just cast out of people will often try to attack the leader. As a result, a leader's faith and self-control must remain strong, especially under pressure.

Leaders often pour out everything they have to others, only to be betrayed and hurt by the people they love. People will quickly turn against you if you preach something they don't like. They did the same to Jesus. One moment they were glorifying Him, and the next, they were yelling, "Crucify Him" (Luke 23:21). After countless painful attacks and built-up hurt, many leaders are wounded, especially in the church. I have experienced my share of hurt over the years and still had to function in ministry because a high demand was placed upon me. I had to pray for my heart to be pure and ask God to heal my broken heart so I could do the assignment. I refused to be a wounded leader, broken and spewing hurt on those I cross paths with.

A wounded leader is someone in leadership that has injured feelings, scars from past experiences, and damage to their soul. Does this definition sound like you? I was a wounded leader, and God sat me down for a season. Things started to dry up, and it felt like I was stagnant in so many areas. I endured so many attacks and almost gave up doing what God called me to do. I will go into greater detail as we go further along in this book. I can now glorify God that I am writing from a place of deliverance to help others who may be hurting. You may feel like this book may not be for you because you don't consider yourself a leader, don't have a title, or preach from behind a pulpit. However, you may still be a leader on some level because a leader commands a group, organization, or country. This definition of leadership means that if you are a parent, sibling, supervisor, or have people looking up to you in some form, you are a leader. Think about it. Regardless of the size of the group, you are a leader. Many people get caught up in comparison of size or total numbers and end up feeling like they aren't leaders because their ministry or sphere of influence is smaller than others. No matter who we are leading, the key is to avoid becoming wounded in the process.

You must stand firm under pressure, but remember to lean on God for strength, especially during difficult times. Will you have to minister to those who hurt you? Absolutely. We can't take it personally. We must become like Jesus when He prayed for those who crucified Him. In upcoming chapters, I will share testimonies of how I had to pray for those who've hurt me. They will never know the severity of the pain they caused because I chose to love and forgive them. You will have to do the same.

As we cover the topics below, strategies for healing, deliverance, and prayer will be provided to ensure your freedom from being a wounded leader.

- Offense
- Competition
- Division
- Curses
- Pride
- Loneliness
- Betrayal
- Rejection
- Dishonor
- Opportunism
- Abandonment (Forgotten)

If you are ready to walk in victory, know that God is prepared to bring you healing. Remember *Psalm 147:3* as you read each page inside this book. *"God heals the brokenhearted and binds up their wounds."* I declare that healing is your portion, and you will no longer be wounded.

CHAPTER 1

Offense

According to the Oxford Dictionary, an offense is the feeling of being resentful or annoyed, typically due to a perceived insult.

Matthew 24:10 says, "And then shall many be offended, and shall betray one another, and shall hate one another."

Jesus warned us that offense would come. Here, He was warning His disciples about the things to come.

An offense will cause you to be annoyed at someone's presence because you feel they attacked you in some way. The spirit of offense is a big problem in the church. People have offended each other since the Biblical days. If you have caused people to get offended at you, for righteous sake, be encouraged. It doesn't mean you are doing something wrong, but you are doing something right. During Jesus' ministry assignment, people became offended at Him for no legitimate reason. Perhaps they felt insecure or jealous. Maybe they didn't understand the power of God that rested on Him, so their hearts became offended. They were blinded to the fact that God sent Him to bless them, so they no longer had to live in bondage (Luke 4:18). Offense blinds and prevents one from receiving from that person's mantle that God is using.

Matthew 13:54 says, "And when he was come into his own country, he taught them in their synagogue, insomuch that they were astonished, and said, Whence hath this man this wisdom, and these mighty works?"

Matthew 13:57 says, "And they were offended in him. But Jesus said unto them, A prophet is not without honour, save in his own country, and in his own house."

Jesus was teaching the Word of God, moving in the miraculous, and the people were offended. Why? They allowed the devil to enter their hearts. Every time we get offended by someone who did no wrong to us because of a false insult, we have allowed the enemy to enter our hearts. We must ask God daily to create a pure heart in us (Psalm 51:10).

I understand how it feels to have a spirit of offense and cause others to be offended at me. I remember one day reaching out to an apostle. I said, "Apostle, do I carry the spirit of offense because people are becoming offended by me because of every little thing?" She took a few minutes to respond because she went into prayer. She replied, "No, be encouraged because the truth offends."

I was glad to hear her response because moments before, I was repenting before God and inquiring about the cause of the constant cycle of offense in my ministry. I couldn't wrap my mind around how people who used to be supporters of what I was doing now became my enemies. They went from speaking well of me to dishonoring and cursing me. These were people who

I mentored and believed in when no one gave them a chance. I vouched for them and thrust them forward. I never expected anything in return, but to learn that they became offended by the message God gave me to preach hurt deeply. I knew something was wrong because on numerous occasions, they stopped coming around. When I reached out to check on them, they no longer took my phone calls. They even unfriended and blocked me on social media. In my heart, I knew I had not done anything wrong to these people, and I still cared for and loved them deeply, regardless of whether their feelings concerning me had changed.

I never cursed them or spoke evil of them, even if others came to me concerning them. I never wanted the public to know the scope of the problem because it was none of their business. Some people operated in the wrong spirit and loved gossip. I never wanted the platform God gave me to be one of slander, drama, or chaos. I took the issue to God, blessed the offended people, and let it go as I released it from my spirit. It took multiple prayer sessions at times, but God is faithful to heal and deliver.

One day, one of my mentees got offended during a mentorship class. She stopped attending the class, and when I called her to ask if everything was okay, she made up excuses such as, "I am busy. I am working double shifts. I lost track of time, etc." Weeks passed, she even had a photo shoot with my husband and we met in person for the first time and she still held onto the offense that she had towards me. Her affection towards me changed, but she didn't want to tell me that she was offended until I confronted her about it.

One evening, I called her and said, "I feel like you are offended with me." She started crying and confessed. "I was so embarrassed. I felt like you were talking about me during class, and I couldn't take it." I replied, "Oh no. I don't do mess. The Lord spoke through me to say whatever came out of my mouth. I don't throw rocks behind the pulpit. So many women in the course might be going through the same thing as you. I'm not sure why you would ever think I could tell your business in such a way. I am terrified of hurting God's people. I am sorry that I have caused an offense and hurt you. It wasn't intentional. I believe what you are feeling may be related to some previous hurts from the last ministry you were a part of."

The young lady agreed that she was dealing with church hurt and had some distrust of women in ministry. I encouraged her to be open to kingdom relationships that God sent. I encouraged her to not allow brokenness and her perspective of women to cause distrust, resulting in her isolation. Two years went by, and she began to come back around. I held no hard feelings toward her. If she ever needs prayer, I am open to serving her.

Around this time, another young lady became offended at me. During our first phone call, she said, "I don't trust women. I don't have any friends. I keep to myself." I said, "I can understand how you feel because I used to be the same way, but God put a love in my heart towards women in ministry. I desire to help them." For weeks, I spent hours on the phone with her, comforting her during her crying spells and helping her navigate her family trauma. While helping my husband photograph a wedding, I spent the entire setup time talking with her on the phone until my husband gave me the signal that he needed my full attention.

One day, I preached a message, and this same lady became upset. During the message, I said, "Oh, I feel the spirit of offense. Don't get offended at me." I didn't think anything of it but continued preaching because those words about offense were a word of knowledge (1 Cor. 12). A few days passed, and I made rounds calling some of my mentees. When I called this young lady, she answered the phone with an attitude. I was shocked. Gone was her kindness. I said, "Is something wrong?" "Yes!" she snapped. "What's wrong?" I asked. "You preached about me during your message."

I said, "No. I don't operate like that. The message God told me to preach applies to many people, including myself." "Well, I can tell you exactly where you said something about me. Go to the forty five-minute mark on the teaching." "Okay," I replied. I hung up the phone. Immediately, I went to the time mark in the audio message where the young lady told me I preached against her. When I heard what she was referring to, I was confused because I didn't understand how she could think I was possibly preaching against her. I know that God is not the author of confusion and that the enemy was playing on her mind.

James 3:16 says, "For where envying and strife is, there is confusion and every evil work."

I sent the lady a kind email. I apologized for causing her hurt and told her that the enemy was playing on her mind, to distrust me because God was using me to help usher deliverance into her life. She responded and told me to give her time to think things over. Weeks went by, and one day, she sent a long email apologizing. God had shown her that she was overwhelmed by hurt from some family relationships. I accepted the apology but had already released her from my spirit. I wasn't focused on her and moved forward in my ministry assignment. I truly cared for this young lady, and dealing with this level of confusion almost made me not want to mentor anyone else. God encouraged me through prayer and fasting, calling me to continue to pour into women. He gave me a strategy to change the order of my training so women could get the healing they needed.

Offense can be vicious if not dealt with immediately. One lady who boldly proclaimed that she was one of my biggest ministry supporters became offended by me. She felt like she should have been next to be called on to serve in my ministry because she had been with me for years. When I asked others to serve and not her, an offense set in her heart. It got out of control. This individual became very critical, and I could do nothing right in her eyes. She felt every post or video was about her. If I sent a nice message to her after taking a few days of prayer to ensure I was in the right spirit, she found a way to take offense by my words. I ended up asking this lady to leave the ministry after doing things according to the Matthew 18:15-17 principle. I spoke to her privately. The tension between us still wasn't resolved. I, then, got a witness involved, and things still were sour. This entire situation humbled me because it led me into constant prayer.

We can't get caught up in the praises of men. The same anointing that caused people to like you will be the same anointing that causes people to hate you. The anointing attracts, but it also repels. When looking at Jesus' ministry, people were with Him one day, and when the opportune moment came, they all deserted him (Mark 14:50). When this individual tried to speak ill of me, it didn't work. God continued to prosper me.

During one conversation, I explained to this young lady that God highlights the people to serve in the ministry, and that's who I ask to serve. We must realize that if we have to force things such as preaching, then we aren't ready. There are some character flaws and imperfections that God wants to work out in us first. He does this so we don't go around hurting others by causing destruction. When the time is right, God will open doors that no one can shut. Occasionally, I still contact this young lady for professional reasons. I still love this person and have forgiven them. I truly pray they will prosper and get the deliverance that Jesus Christ provided by His blood that was shed for us.

In the past, I have been offended at others and went from supporting them to no longer being interested in what they had to say. I have a Christian Magazine *(Rejoice Essential Magazine)* that comes with much rejection. I often wondered why God gave it to me. I have been stood up, lied to, and ignored when trying to schedule interviews with various ministers. I wanted to quit many times, but the Holy Spirit never allowed me to. One day, I was washing dishes, and the Holy Spirit revealed that the reason I didn't care for this individual that I used to listen to preach was that I got offended at them. It was like a light bulb moment, and I repented. I binded up the spirit of offense and blessed this person. It took some time and much prayer. Shortly after, I saw something this preacher posted on social media and wasn't annoyed. I knew that God had delivered me.

Another time, a pastor wanted to connect with me and asked to come on my platform for us to minister together. It was supposed to be a tag team video where we delivered the message back and forth. However, this person just took over, and I couldn't even get a word in. I immediately felt offended and frustrated inside, and shut down. It was so awful that I couldn't even finish my sentences. I was on a LIVE broadcast, and I made sure my facial expression didn't show how I truly felt. I was looking forward to the broadcast to end. After the broadcast ended, this individual told me I needed to learn how to flow. I didn't respond but simply told the pastor, "God bless you and I will speak with you later." I thought, "How can I flow when I can't even talk without you interrupting?" I didn't receive those words because they were not true. Every time I minister, I am flowing with the Holy Spirit. Even when I don't try to prophesy, it flows out of me. I never try to shine a spotlight on myself; honestly, I prefer to stay hidden. Monday through Friday, I labor in prayer with other intercessors on the prayer line, and there are too many miracles to count. When this pastor spoke those words, I knew the enemy was trying to get me to be offended. This person had invited me to be one of the speakers at their church's conference. I almost messaged this person to tell them, "I can't preach for you at your conference. Please count me out." But the Holy Spirit stopped me.

We must be open to the Holy Spirit and realize that He flows differently through each person according to His preference. We don't have to be aggressive or rude in our approach to ministering. We need interview etiquette and be careful not to offend the host when you come on their platform. When we get on camera or a LIVE video, there are dos and don'ts. If you are thirsty for an opportunity and aren't used to being on camera, it will show up on camera. You can become prideful, boastful, and very assertive. We must be kind and honorable to the host of the broadcast. To get over the offense with this pastor, I went into prayer to release it. God showed me that this person was truly excited about coming on a larger platform than theirs and meant nothing by it. I began to pray for this pastor and bless them. How can I become offended by someone that I am praying for? The main reason we become offended easily by people is that we aren't praying for them. After I got out of prayer, I sent a cash app to sow into the pastor's ministry.

I refused to allow the devil to plant seeds of offense in me and become a hypocrite when I stand before people to preach the Word of God. That pastor and I speak often, and there is no offense in my heart concerning them.

DANGERS

1. Offense not dealt with can cause bitterness.
2. Offense can cause you to be critical of others, attacking those God sent to help you.
3. If your leader, who has the heart of God concerning you, tells you something, don't get offended. Obey because they keep watch over your souls (Hebrews 13:17).
4. Offense will tear ministries apart.
5. Offense will cause you to be too prideful to receive.

6. Offense will block your blessings. God uses people to bless you. Where there is no honor, it will be harder to receive from the people that God is using. Remember, Jesus couldn't do many miracles in His hometown because of the lack of honor (Matthew 13:57).
7. Offense causes distrust.

SOLUTION

1. Ask God to create in you a pure heart. Let the offense go. Don't allow the offense to fester into bitterness and hate.
2. Instead of looking at the log in others' eyes, look at the plank in your eyes (Matthew 7:3-5). Allow God to work on you and your shortcomings before you try to point out others.
3. Pray that you have a teachable spirit. So, when your leadership corrects you, there will be no pride in you, and you can obey what the Lord is speaking through them. For instance, if they say you aren't ready to preach, maybe God is showing them some character flaws in you that need to be perfected. Don't get ahead of God because you will be out of season.
4. If you have become offended by a minister, pray for them instead of gossiping and spreading discord on social media. The Body of Christ must be unified.
5. People often become offended by the one God sent them to learn from. Look at how the disciples in the Bible took rebuke from Jesus. They were often rebuked for having a lack of faith (Matthew 8:26), yet they still received of Jesus. We must humble ourselves and not allow offense to set in when leadership rebukes us so we can improve.
6. Offense will cause disconnections of kingdom relationships from those God sent in your life. Many people have disconnected from those important relationships due to offense, and now they find themselves trying to compete against them.

7. Offended people lose trust in everybody. They lose the respect, trust, and esteem they had for leadership. Instead of addressing them by their title, such as pastor or prophetess, they start calling that person by their government name, "Kim, Mike, Troy, etc."

DECLARATIONS

Lord, I refuse to walk in offense in Jesus' name.

Lord, create in me a pure heart so the spirit of offense doesn't rule in me.

Lord, I cast down any offense that wants to be planted in me, and I surrender all the pain to You.

Lord, I forgive my offender in Jesus' name.

Lord, I bless the person who has offended me in Jesus' name.

Lord, help me to move past the offense and put love in my heart for the offender in Jesus' name.

Lord, deliver and set me free.

Lord, send Your purifying fire to get anything out of me that is not of You.

CHAPTER 2

Competition

According to Merriam-Webster Dictionary, the meaning of the word COMPETING is in a state of rivalry or competition (as for position, profit, or a prize). We all have been guilty of wanting to win a game, title, or position, but it's all about our motives. If we have the wrong motives, then we will not please God. In the world, people are always trying to "keep up with the Jones" or outdo one another. However, we must be unified in the Body of Christ and realize that we are one body with many members (1 Corinthians 12:12-27). We must know our assignment from God and not get outside of His will. Some people may not see that competition is bad because it's in the Bible, but many leaders are wounded because of it. Apostle Paul compares our faith walk to a competition.

2 Timothy 2:5 says, "An athlete is not crowned unless he competes according to the rules."

1 Corinthians 9:24 says, "Do you not know that in a race all the runners run, but only one receives the prize? So run that you may obtain it."

These scriptures refer to our faith walk being a marathon, not a sprint. We must fight to get to the end so we can receive the crown of life as we enter into glory with our Lord. We are fighting against the enemy who is constantly seeking to kill, steal, and destroy us (John 10:10). These scriptures are not about competing against our brothers and sisters in Christ. God's heart is for the Body of Christ to be unified because Jesus prayed that we would walk in unity before His crucifixion (John 17:11). How can we be unified if we compete against one another? It will be a hard task. Look at the scriptures below. Notice the word "rivalries."

Galatians 5:19-20 (ESV) says, "Now the works of the flesh are evident: sexual immorality, impurity, sensuality, idolatry, sorcery, enmity, strife, jealousy, fits of anger, rivalries, dissensions, divisions."

Rivalry is another word for competition. When we rival against our brother and sister in Christ, we are in the flesh, not the Spirit (Galatians 5:16-26). Our flesh is not led by God's Spirit. Let's look at another scripture with the word "rivalry."

Philippians 2:3 says, "Do nothing from rivalry or conceit, but in humility count others more significant than yourselves."

Before you do anything, ask yourself, "Am I doing this to compete against someone?" If your answer is yes, then you are operating in the flesh and God is not pleased with your actions because you are going against His Word. Why do people compete with one another? Envy! Look at the scripture below.

Galatians 5:26 says, "Let us not become conceited, provoking one another, envying one another."

We are told not to envy one another. We are not supposed to covet what they have, resent them, and strive to take over what they have. Yet many people in the Body of Christ are doing this exact thing, and many are hurting from the pew to the pulpit.

I have poured into many for years, only to be kicked to the curb when people felt like I no longer had any value. It took me a while to process that people come and go in our lives, but the hurtful thing is when those very people are now competing against me. God is a true healer and has helped me keep going. The following testimonies aren't to bash anyone but to simply illustrate the principles in God's Word.

One day, an individual in leadership in my ministry started to conspire against me. Every time I got around them, I felt an uneasy feeling inside of me, and I couldn't figure out the source of these feelings, and that we just couldn't fully connect. I believe it was the Holy Spirit revealing the person's intentions. Some elders approached me about this individual and told me how they discerned that this person had the wrong motives. I listened to them and prayed it through but continued to fellowship with the person.

Months went by, and I started watching this person on social media. I could see them working my pages. They weren't on my page because it was a blessing to them; they were on my page to promote themselves. They told people to follow them and that their ministry was higher than mine. After much prayer, I decided to cut off access with the individual. I love them very much, but we must be good stewards of our ministries. We can't allow any spirit to come in and cause havoc regardless of who the devil is using.

This individual lied to my face. "Prophetess, I will never do a prayer call at the same time you are doing yours," they said. Yet, that's exactly what happened. Once they left the ministry, they started recruiting people from my ministry and doing events simultaneous to mine. This person would look on my social media page for inspiration instead of going to God. It was as if they wanted to take my ministry. If you do events or meetings because you saw someone else doing it and haven't prayed, God is not in it. This person was trying to replicate everything I was doing.

I received word that this person had puffed themselves up. They were boasting, "My classes and ministry are higher than Prophetess K's." Here was pride manifesting, and some were too blind to notice. If you must boast about yourself to influence others, you are operating in pride. The Bible tells us to allow others to boast about us and not ourselves.

Proverbs 27:2 (NKJV) says, "Let another man praise you, and not your own mouth; A stranger, and not your own lips."

I couldn't believe I was dealing with an Absalom spirit, the epitome of competition. Absalom was King David's son. In 2 Samuel 15:2-6, Absalom started to conspire against his father by telling people to come to him instead. He won the people over, and they started to bow before him. When they bowed, he took their hands and kissed them to show that he was their equal. Shortly after, Absalom made his move to take David's Kingdom.

As I was going through this situation, I thought, "God, why doesn't this individual trust you to send the people instead of trying to divide this ministry?" I searched myself and repented for anything that could've allowed this situation. I have never gone to someone's ministry and caused division. The strategy of the enemy is to divide and destroy. I just shook my head and blessed this individual. Sometimes, warfare happens because we are on the right path, and the devil will try to cause distractions or derail our assignment.

Some preach, "People aren't your sheep but Jesus' sheep. They can go where they want." Yes, while that is true, many skip the part where God is a God of order and rebellion is the sin of witchcraft. God put His chosen vessel in charge when He gave them the mandate. He didn't give the person in competition or the one rebelling against leadership the mandate. The rebellious person is operating illegally because they are doing something God never authorized. The rebellious person is working witchcraft because they divide a church and recruit sheep into their ministry that God hasn't ordained. For instance, God authorized David to be King, not Absalom. As a result, Absalom was outside of God's will and died prematurely. Sin equals death, and staying in God's will is the safest place to be. When we are in God's will, He can protect us. It is God's heart to see people added to the church. In the Book of Acts, people were added to the church daily and sometimes by the thousands as the disciples went out to preach.

Many leaders have dealt with an Absalom spirit and haven't moved past it. There is hope and restoration for you. God eventually sent double the people who left my ministry and rebuilt me in every way possible. My social media exploded. God sent deals for me to make multiple income streams, increase my income streams, and influence on my life. He gave me double for my trouble because I refused to grow bitter about what that individual did to me. Every time I cut the camera on, I get paid, and I give God the glory. God will compensate you for all the pain you endured. Just hold tight.

Another way we compete against each other in the Body of Christ is having a lack of support. Leaders need our support. Moses had Aaron, Hur, and Miriam. David had Nathan and Gad. So many leaders are depressed and discouraged because of feelings of lack of support. When they do LIVE teachings, where are the people from their ministry? When they do events, barely anyone shows up. After laboring and putting together books, music, products, etc., where are the customers? Instead of supporting someone who is a laborer of the Gospel, we try to compete against them. We think, "Oh, they wrote a book. Well, I will write two books." Our first instinct should be, "Congratulations on your book. Let me get a copy." However, many won't support them because they may be jealous and feel they need to compete to validate their pride.

I often have felt discouraged and wanted to give up because of the lack of support. I knew God gave me an idea or told me to do something. I obeyed, but then I felt disappointed by those I led trying to undermine my ministry efforts. I invited them months in advance, but they had the mindset to copy my endeavors and plan an event at the same time as mine. If we had partnered, it would have benefited both of us. I released that person from my spirit and received God's peace. You must do the same for those who were once a part of your ministry, but now they are attempting to compete with you.

Pride and competition will prevent supporting one another. Those who are prideful need the spotlight. They don't feel comfortable when the Spirit of God flows through someone else. They need to hear the praises of men for their egos. Some people won't support you because they are threatened by your presence or gifts, and they feel like you are going to take over. People are trying to out-preach, out-sing, out-worship, out-write, etc., each other, and God is not being glorified. We must be comfortable in our own skin and know our purpose to stop competing with our brothers and sisters in Christ. Many times, we hear prideful ministers tearing down another preacher because they have a smaller following. They fail to realize that every person isn't called to have a mega-church; some may lead a storefront. The size of our ministries doesn't determine the size of our anointing. God can use us powerfully in a small ministry to cast out devils and heal the sick, while in a mega-church, there may not be any signs.

Competition doesn't just come from your mentees or members, but it can come from your peers. Our peers can covet what you have and compete against you. However, you must know that God gave you the assignment, so oil is on it. You are anointed for the task and protected by the Father. We will have Heaven's backing when we are in God's will. Some of my peers weren't even doing prayer calls when we first met. One individual who wanted to connect with me set up their prayer call at the same time as mine and started inviting people who were a part of my ministry.

Another time, a prophet invited me to preach at her event only to compete with me. She looked at my social media following and felt I could draw a crowd. When I arrived at the service, she insisted on being on the microphone while I was speaking. I'm not sure why she felt like she needed to have a microphone as well. I'm soft- spoken and her voice was thunderous. As I went forth, she was on the mic yelling, "Go, prophetess." It was awful for me and a major distraction to everyone else. She wanted to be seen. I put down the microphone and went around the room and put my mouth to the people's ears, and spoke as loudly as I could without hurting their eardrum. After service, I was in the lobby and overheard her asking about me and what I was ministering to the people. She didn't know I was listening. This prophet was trying to check if the prophecies I gave were accurate. I heard this lady that I didn't know to testify, "Wow! She was very accurate. She knew I was in a Newspaper and more." Many times, people will invite you places but then vie for attention in your midst. They don't want to allow the Spirit of God to flow fully in you. We must receive the gift of the man or woman of God when they come without our interference. We must do our research to feel comfortable letting them flow as the Holy Spirit leads. We need to sit down and receive their ministry because so many leaders pour out and never get poured into.

DANGERS:

1. Competition will cause you to speak evil and ill will about someone.
2. Competition will reveal the jealousy hidden in your heart.
3. Competition stems from insecurity.
4. Competition will cause you to miss out on your true assignment.
5. Competition is flesh led.
6. Competition results in wrong and un-pure motives.
7. Competition puffs one up in pride.
8. Competition causes one to be distracted by the enemy.

SOLUTIONS:

1. Pray for those who try to compete with you instead of speaking evil about them. Don't curse them, but bless them. Imagine if the shoe was on the other foot. Do you want people to do to you what you are doing to others?
2. Stay focused on Jesus. If we are focused on Jesus, we will have perfect peace (Isaiah 26:3). We will develop a heart of love for God's people, and the Holy Spirit can deal with our hearts in a greater measure.
3. Avoid social media until you get delivered. Just because you have been waiting for God to bless you in a way as He is blessing others, wait for your turn. Rejoice for other's accomplishments and be a supporter, not a hater.
4. Support others. It's okay to like the status of others on social media, share their videos, go to their events, and get their products. We should often be gleaning from the person, not competing against them. Don't do what they are doing unless you have God's instructions. You don't want to miss out on what God has for you to do because you are copying someone else's assignment.

5. Realize that there is work for all of us to do. You will be busy once you know what you are supposed to be doing. Ministry work is 24/7. It never stops. Our brothers and sisters in Christ are not our competition.

6. Seek God for instructions on what you should be doing. He can't protect you if you get outside of God's will. You want to be anointed for the assignment so you can handle the warfare that comes with it. With this anointing, you will have the grace for that particular mandate.

DECLARATIONS

Lord, I will not operate in competitiveness.

Lord, get any insecurity, jealousy, and envy out of me in Jesus' name.

Lord, bless me with the right motives for why I am doing something.

Lord, bless me to have an ear to hear what You are saying to the church.

Lord, let me stay in Your will so I know my assignment.

Lord, bless me to know my purpose in life.

Lord, bless me to support others in Jesus' name.

Lord, order and guide my steps.

Lord, I yield my desires and flesh to you, and I pick up Your agenda.

Lord, don't let me be distracted by the enemy in Jesus' name.

CHAPTER 3

Division

Division has caused a lot of damage in the Body of Christ. Too many differences have caused friction, church splits, and wounded people who truly need deliverance. Once experienced, some don't know how to move forward. We expect the world to be divided because certain systems are in place such as a divided government (Democratic or Republican), neighborhoods (e.g. New York City neighborhoods or even burrows are delineated by the ethnicities of its residents), and continents (There are seven continents: Europe, Asia, Australia, Antarctica, North America, South America, and Africa).

The point is that the spirit of division has infiltrated the world around us and so it is not surprising that the church, since the Bible age, has also dealt with the spirit of division. In the New Testament, we read about how Jesus first came for the Jews, and when they rejected Him, He made salvation available to all including the Gentiles or non-Jews (Romans 1:16, Acts 13:46). As a result, some of the disciples didn't care too much for the Gentiles until the Holy Spirit instructed them to preach the Gospel to every living creature. One day Apostle Peter had a visitation, and was instructed to go to Cornelius' (a Gentile) house, and the Lord moved mightily. People were saved, baptized, and started to speak in tongues when they heard the Gospel of Jesus Christ preached (Acts 10).

Some people aren't open to what God wants to do and have allowed division to harden their hearts. Whether Jews or Gentiles, we are saved by faith in Jesus Christ when we believe that God raised Him from the dead on the third day (Ephesians 2:8, Romans 10:9).

During the 2020 presidential election, many prophets prophesied based on their political viewpoint. If they were a Democrat they would prophesy Joe Biden would win, and contrarily, if they were a Republican, they would prophesy that Donald Trump would win. Even though Joe Biden became the 46th president of the United States, some of the prophets who prophesied that he would win weren't under the inspiration of the Holy Spirit when they released the prophecy. They were in their flesh and wanted to make an accurate prediction for fame. The Lord knew the hearts of the prophets, so He allowed a lying spirit to enter into the church to expose the motives of men. Remember, we are on the Lord's side, and can't afford to get caught up in division.

2 Thessalonians 2:11 says, "And for this cause God shall send them strong delusion, that they should believe a lie."

Sadly, many were also under a strong delusion and didn't want to believe the fact that Donald Trump had lost the election. Some became even more prideful and started operating in witchcraft as they prayed against Joe Biden. We aren't supposed to curse but to bless (Romans 12:14). We are supposed to pray for leaders (1 Timothy 2:2). It doesn't matter who is King or President because Jesus is still on the throne. His reign doesn't stop based on the outcome of an election. Many people realized the error of their ways, repented, drew closer to the Lord and allowed God to get their hearts back into true alignment with Him.

We are commanded to love one another because the Bible says both to love God with our whole heart, soul, and mind and to love our neighbors as ourselves (Matthew 22:37-39). Yet, the enemy comes in and causes division by trivial matters such as the foods we eat, how we should dress, and if we have certain spiritual gifts. Romans 14:13-23 tells us not to be divided by such things but to unify and not judge others. We are all brothers and sisters in Christ. If we believe in Jesus, then we should really stand together.

When I first got saved, I attended a church that taught women couldn't wear pants. We couldn't eat catfish or shrimp because they are bottom feeders. We couldn't wear jewelry, makeup, or trim our hair. If we did such things, then we were looked down upon. This was a Holiness or an Apostolic denomination and they based their theological foundation on the teaching from Acts 2. Some of the things that divided us are trivial indeed.

As we explore church history, we can see in Galatians 2:11-14 how the enemy tried to divide Apostle Paul and Apostle Peter. Both of these men moved in the miraculous. Peter's shadow healed the sick (Acts 5:15). Paul would impart the anointing into a handkerchief to heal the sick (Acts 19:11-12). However, Peter had an aversion to Paul because he wasn't one of the original twelve disciples who walked with Jesus. We should not imitate the actions of Peter. We must not be hypocritical in our actions and miss what the Lord is doing in our midst. We might not care too much about the person God is using, but we can not tell God what to do? He is all-powerful and sovereign. It's better to be in His will and agenda than to stand against Him.

Dr. Martin Luther King, civil rights activist and preacher, once said that Sunday morning is the most segregated hour in America. He dreamed about a day where Whites and Blacks could come together in society without hatred. The devil has filled many hearts to discriminate against an individual's skin color, worship practices, musical preferences, and the level of demonstration in the Body of Christ. There are so many denominations in the church with differing theological perspectives.

Many have read about the Azusa Street Revival that was started by a Black man named William Seymour. He was hungry for God and went to bible school. Because of Jim Crow laws during this time, he wasn't allowed to sit in the classroom with all of his white peers. He had to sit outside with a paper bag on his head. God chose the least likely person to steward a revival during the early 1900s. This revival caused racial boundaries to be crossed despite Jim Crow laws. An organization called Pentecostal Assemblies of the World (P.A.W.) formed as a result of this revival. Despite this powerful movement, the enemy came in and caused division in this organization many times.

The first split was caused by Whites not wanting to be accountable to a black leader; as a result, they formed the Assemblies of God organization. The Assemblies of God organization, to this day, is predominately white. Another time, the P.A.W. split to form the Church of God in Christ (COGIC) founded by C.H. Mason. The Apostolic or Holiness church I attended was a part of the P.A.W. Every month, our P.A.W. church would gather for church service with another local church, considered our sister church, from the Assemblies of God. When we gathered, I watched how different members from both sides made slick comments about the choice of song, the way someone danced, or the tone of the praise. We weren't truly unified.

2 Corinthians 5:16 says, "From now on, therefore, we regard no one according to the flesh..."

The verse above is a reminder to stop viewing people from a fleshly point of view. Can you recognize the anointing on their life? God can flow however He chooses. Our minds have been brainwashed to the point where we can't recognize the anointing of the Holy Ghost. Some people believe if a preacher isn't hollering or hooping, then they aren't operating under the anointing. Some don't believe in women preachers. Others don't believe God can use people who think or flow differently. Kathryn Kuhlman was soft-spoken, performed many miracles, and filled up stadiums. She was an evangelist who passed away in 1976 and known as a faith healer. We can be loud or soft and still have a move of God. We can be male or female, and God can use us powerfully. We can be Black, White, Hispanic, Indian, Asian, etc., and God can use us in the miraculous. We must learn not to get offended by the moves of God and appreciate His plans and purposes.

Some have blasphemed the Holy Ghost by speaking against moves of His Spirit that they didn't understand. Some have said the gifts of the Spirit (1 Corinthians 12:4-11) were demonic because they didn't have that gift operating in them or lacked the understanding. We must be cautious about speaking against God.

When I attended the Holiness church, we were very divided regarding methods of baptism. We taught people and even told them to their faces that if they weren't baptized in the name of Jesus they were going to hell. There are two scriptures that I want to highlight about how we should conduct baptism. One says to baptize in the name of the Lord "Jesus," and the other says to baptize in the Father, the Son, and the Holy Spirit.

Acts 2:38 says, "Then Peter said unto them, Repent, and be baptized every one of you in the name of Jesus Christ for the remission of sins, and ye shall receive the gift of the Holy Ghost."

Matthew 28:19 says, "Go ye therefore, and teach all nations, baptizing them in the name of the Father, and of the Son, and of the Holy Ghost:"

I didn't realize how I was shaking someone's faith by planting seeds that they weren't saved and not permitted into Heaven because of the way they were baptized. I never want to be a stumbling block to someone's salvation or weaken someone who is a babe in Christ. I have learned over the years that people will believe what they want to and do what they have been taught. So it's better to baptize in both ways "in Jesus' name" and "the Father, the Son, and the Holy Spirit." When I got my children baptized, this is how my previous apostle did it as he dipped my daughter and son beneath the water.

So many leaders are wounded because someone may sown discord in their church. They thought the person was for them or gave them a trusted position, only to be stabbed in the back. They are hurting also because some of their members left their ministry to follow after those who initiated division. I can relate because someone I esteemed divided my ministry, and a flood of emotions gripped my heart. I was disappointed but as time went on, the Lord brought healing to my heart, and I was no longer upset.

Some leaders are dividing the church due to pride and selfishness. Perhaps they feel envious of a position that a pastor assigned to someone else. When the person didn't get what they wanted, they left upset. Maybe they talked badly about the ministry and took some of the current members with them. Out of anger and offense, they may have started their own church. The new church may have seemed to thrive for a season, but the foundation was built erroneously. It wasn't built because God instructed them to do so, but rather, out of pain, pride, offense, and selfish ambitions as the root cause.

Unless the Lord builds the house, those that labor do so in vain. If we are building in vain, then we don't have God's approval, and He can't bless us. For instance, it doesn't matter how immaculate a house is and how much someone renovates it for more curb appeal. If there is a crack or damage to the foundation, the house will have sorts of problems and be structurally unstable, causing other issues with the roof, doors, windows increasingly over time. The same applies to us as we build our own ministry. If we become upset, split a church because we weren't being used in that ministry, and start our own ministry out of rejection without getting the Lord's approval, then we open ourselves to problems later on. Instead of growth, we will see our ministry split over again when we reach a certain level. It is the principle of reaping what we have sown.

If we see a divisive person, then we should warn them of their harmful practices. If they don't take heed, then it is necessary to cut ties with them or the spirit of division will run rampant in the church (Romans 16:17-18). Divisive people can be dangerous because they split churches, friendships, homes, etc. Whether you have been divisive or been a victim of the spirit of division, there is healing and deliverance for you.

DANGERS

1. Unforgiveness
2. Church splits
3. Hurt (leaders don't want to grow anymore)
4. Being led by the flesh

SOLUTION

1. Forgive
2. Resist the devil, shun gossip, and guard your heart
3. Don't quit your assignment. Realize that people come and go. Stand firm.
4. Be led by God's Spirit in everything.

DECLARATIONS

Lord, if I have caused division in the church, please forgive me.

Lord, I repent of allowing myself to have the wrong motives.

Lord, if something is not of you, please, get it out of me in Jesus' name.

Lord, I don't want to be prideful, offended, or have the wrong motives.

Lord, if I have to leave a ministry, allow me to do so tastefully.

Lord, bless me never to put my mouth on your people to gossip about them.

Lord, uproot any divisive spirit from my life, ministry, and home in Jesus' name.

Lord, purify my heart, motives, and my mind in Jesus' name.

Lord, bless those I may have hurt through the spirit of division.

Lord, heal my heart from any trauma that division may have caused.

CHAPTER 4

Curses

Curses are ill-spoken words spoken against someone. Curses are also wishing that something bad happens to someone. Witches, workers of darkness, and some people in the church have cursed one another. When people get mad that someone is prospering, they curse them by praying against their success. They want them to die prematurely and stumble in their ways. It's demonic when we rejoice when someone falls away from grace into sin. Many have secretly cheered because they envied that person's position. We must know what God has for us is for us. We all have work to do for the Father, and a part to play. We can't afford to allow the devil to enter our hearts to cause us to speak ill of one another. Wounded leaders have cursed those they were threatened by due to their own insecurities and pain. God is looking at our hearts daily, so we have to rid ourselves of anything that's not like Him.

When someone has wronged us, we can't take the bait of cursing them. Often, people have cursed their enemy (a person) when the true enemy is the devil operating in the individual.

Ephesians 6:12 says, "For we wrestle not against flesh and blood, but against principalities, against powers, against rulers of the darkness of this world, against spiritual wickedness in high places."

We must look through the eyes of the spirit and use discernment. The enemy can use people even if they aren't aware of it. Jesus Christ discerned that Satan was speaking through Peter, so He rebuked him (Mark 8:33). The enemy influences the hearts and minds of lost people (2 Corinthians 4:4).

Often, when leaders are hurt, they will curse those who leave their ministry. It may be painful if someone leaves our ministry because we have grown to love and care for them, but we must remember that they are God's sheep. If someone wants to leave our ministry, let them go. If they feel like they have outgrown us, bless them so they can get what they need. Just because someone leaves, we don't have to cut them off, become bitter, and turn others against them. The mature thing to do in Christ is to love and release them. God will fill the void in your heart for the person.

Sometimes, leaders make a mistake in cursing people with cancer, other sicknesses, and failure if they try to leave. They start operating in witchcraft, control, and manipulation. They say, "If you leave this ministry, you won't be prosperous." This is a curse. God delights in our prosperity; we can prosper by being planted in another church. Our job as leaders is to love people where they are and to train, equip, impart, bless, teach, pray, and encourage them. We shouldn't curse a person's destiny if they want to learn elsewhere because no person has everything. We all need one another. There are many gifts in the Body of Christ but one body (1 Corinthians 12:12-27). A leader may be anointed, but they may not be graced in another area compared to someone else.

Over the years, I have prayed, fasted, and grown to care for many. I remember spending hours on the phone counseling this married couple because they wanted a divorce. It was exhausting, but I made myself available to help them. Unfortunately, this same couple decided to leave my ministry. I was sad, but I released a blessing over them. I didn't cut them off. I told them if they ever needed anything, then my door was always open. However, many are wounded, and they cut the person off entirely and speak ill of them. If we operate in God's love, we must renew our minds and realize that some people are seasonal. Some will be with us for the long haul. People will come and go, and perhaps our purpose in that person's life was fulfilled.

Romans 12:14 says, "Bless those that persecute you and not curse them."

Persecution doesn't feel good, but we can't take it personally. We are being persecuted for righteousness' sake, and our persecutors are lost and need our prayers. If Jesus can pray for His crucifiers on the cross in His agony (Luke 23:34), then how much more you and I? When we are hurt, our flesh wants others to hurt, but this is not God's heart. God is forgiving and merciful. He knows how to judge our enemies but leave the judgment part up to Him. Sometimes, when we get hurt, we want the person to die, suffer, and get what's coming to them. Be careful not to curse.

Once, I was betrayed by someone I care for deeply, so I started planning revenge. I felt murder enter my heart, and I went into prayer angrily. I had no idea the depth of my scorn. I prayed that the Lord's presence cut through all my wounds. When I prayed, "Lord, let them hurt like I hurt," I heard the Holy Spirit instruct me to pray for the person. "Huh?" I replied. Then the Holy Spirit repeated Himself. My flesh didn't want to pray, and I didn't even know what to say. Out of my love for God, I obeyed, and over time, a few seconds of prayer for this person turned into minutes. As weeks passed, I had a love in my heart for this person and truly wanted them to be blessed. Through the disappointments and pain, I continue to bless my enemies and those who hurt me. Miraculously, God took the hatred out and replaced it with His love.

Matthew 5:44 says, "But I say unto you, Love your enemies, bless them that curse you, do good to them that hate you, and pray for them which despitefully use you, and persecute you."

The key in this verse is to love. We may not like someone, but we must love them because God commanded it. When we see our enemies suffering, don't smile and say, "Haha. That's what they get." That's very wicked. There was this individual who talked ill of me, and it came back to me. I never did anything to this person, and it hurt me to find out how they felt. I never approached the person but continued to pray for them and show kindness. Years went by, and this person had a health scare. They remembered me and reached out for prayer. My flesh could have been happy that they were in pain. However, I rebuked any thoughts of payback and humbled myself. I extended God's love to help restore the person's faith, and administered healing through God's healing gifts.

Romans 12:19 (ESV) says, "Beloved, never avenge yourselves, but leave it to the wrath of God, for it is written, "Vengeance is mine, I will repay, says the Lord."

How God decides to judge is up to Him. We may not see the person's judgment today, but years later, it can catch up to them. God is not mocked. People reap where they sow (Galatians 6:7). We should pray for mercy for our enemies because they will need it. If we have God's heart, we will start to feel sorry for our enemies. I feel sorry for this individual when their soul was broken, and they didn't know if they would live to see another year. Leaders must keep on serving without ulterior motives.

1 Peter 3:9 (ESV) says, "Do not repay evil with evil or insult with insult, but with blessing, because to this you were called so that you may inherit a blessing."

Christians must operate differently than witches. They curse, cast spells, and pray for our demise. If we do the opposite and bless others, we will obtain a blessing. Why? It's the principle of sowing and reaping. We reap what we sow. Recently, a lady posted the following on Facebook:

"I went to the doctor and got a bad report that I didn't have much time left. If it's my time to die, then it's just my time. I know this is because I have prayed death on people and it's coming back into my life."

The lady was broken, and she publicly repented. Don't operate in witchcraft, cursing those who have wronged you. Remember, you can't control what others do, but you can control how you respond.

Numbers 23:8 (ESV) says. "How can I curse whom God has not cursed? How can I denounce whom the LORD has not denounced?"

Curse workers forget one thing. They can't curse whom God has blessed. They can try to fast, pray, and do many rituals, but it won't work. No weapon formed against us will prosper. I had people try to release death upon me. Many enemies have gathered together to conspire against me. However, their plans of destruction concerning my life didn't work. Some attacks I've seen with my natural eyes, and others I have seen in the spiritual realm as the Holy Spirit revealed it to me. God knew that I was mature enough to pray a blessing over my enemies and trust Him for His protection.

A few years ago, a scandal arose where a false apostle released death and cancer on people who left his ministry. Years later, he got very sick, fighting for his life. This person would release fear into people and function as a warlock. God doesn't give us the spirit of fear. Perfect love casts out fear. God promised us a long life. God doesn't release sickness upon people because He's a healer.

Many people have used things in the Old Testament as an excuse to curse. However, they miss the point that Jesus turned the other cheek, and we are told to bless, not curse. In Genesis 3, God curses the serpent to crawl on its belly and be underneath man's heels. God also cursed Adam to sweat for his toil and Eve to have pain during childbirth. These curses came as a result of their punishment for disobedience. Their sin caused them to get outside God's will, and His hedge of protection was lifted. God is sovereign. In the New Testament, we are underneath a new dispensation. Jesus' blood has washed away our sins, and God has extended His grace and mercy. God is love, and we are to love one another.

DANGERS

1. Reliance on the devil's tactics
2. Unclean heart
3. Reaping what you sown
4. Operating in the flesh

SOLUTION

1. We can't use the devil's tactics to defeat him. We only defeat the devil through Jesus. We overcome evil with good. Using the devil's ways will unleash demonic spirits in your life.

2. Allow God to heal your heart. No matter how deep the pain, God is a comforter and healer. As you yield to Him, you will overcome the offense.

3. You don't want people to curse you, so don't do it to others. When God starts elevating you, more intercessors are needed to cover you because of new levels, new devils.

4. Be Spirit led, not flesh led. Don't take the bait of allowing your flesh to dominate your actions. Yield to the Holy Spirit and get deliverance so you don't become bitter.

DECLARATIONS

Lord, I will pray for those who have mistreated me.

Lord, I will bless those who have cursed me.

Lord, I will let go of the pain and pray for those who have wronged me.

Lord, deliver me from anything in my heart that's against you and anyone else.

Lord, guard my lips so I can only speak words of edification.

Lord, help me to move past the pain.

Lord, I will let those who want to leave my life leave.

Lord, I will release prayers of blessings on those who want to leave my ministry.

Lord, I am blessed, and the enemy can't curse who is blessed.

Lord, I will love others and serve them unto you.

I am protected by the full armor of God.

CHAPTER 5

Pride

Have you ever known a prideful leader? Pride is one of the lusts of the flesh. Since the beginning of time, the pride of life has manifested itself. Starting with Lucifer, an anointed cherub, who was a worship leader. He wanted to be higher than God, and his toxic behavior got a third of the angels kicked out of Heaven due to pride spreading (Ezekiel 28; Revelation 12).

King Nebuchadnezzar was also a case of prideful leadership. He thought he was god in his own eyes and made a statue and demanded everyone to worship it. However, Shadrack, Meshach, and Abednego refused. This king was very prideful because he didn't want anyone else to advance. He wanted all the glory and was very insecure. As a result, he lost his mind and was doomed to eat grass in the field like a wild ox. Nebuchadnezzar was exiled from his kingdom for seven years until he gave God glory (Daniel 3-4).

Also, there was Nabal, who was married to Abigail. His name means fool. He was indeed foolish, prideful, and selfish. He endangered his whole household by talking disrespectfully to King David and his men. He had enough food and resources to share, but he refused when asked by the king. Nabal's pride and selfishness resulted in his death because his wife confessed that she gave David and his men resources without his knowledge. God ultimately struck Nabal down because of his hard heart (1 Samuel 25).

Lastly, King Saul was a very insecure and a proud leader. He wanted all the praise for himself. He lost his mind when he heard the people singing, *"Saul killed his thousand, but David killed his ten thousand (1 Samuel 18:7)."* From that day, he allowed the devil to rule in his heart to try to kill David. Saul didn't realize that David had blessed his life and kingdom. Pride will blind you from receiving the help that God sent you.

People may start off right in ministry. However, over time, pride can set in if they esteem themselves higher than they ought. There is a correlation between pride and hurt. For instance, someone who has experienced a lot of hurt or disappointment can say, "I will not allow anyone to talk to me like this, or no one can tell me anything." The fact is that they are speaking from a wounded place. Out of the abundance of the heart, the mouth speaks (Luke 6:45).

Pride is often used as a coverup. It is employed as a shield to mask the pain. People may even try to deflect a problem onto others so people won't look at their issues. As a result, they blame others and rarely look at themselves. They fail to realize that God is looking right at the pride in their hearts. Pride can deceive many into believing that they are better than they truly are currently. None of us have arrived, and we all have areas of our lives that we can improve. If we don't spend time with the Lord as we ought, our old ways will start returning. The flesh will start to arise, and the temptation will be at an all-time high. We need to pray without ceasing so we won't be led into temptation. When I spend time with the Holy Spirit, He reveals areas of my life that must be cultivated. He tells me when I handled a situation wrong and the correction needed. He shows me the sin in my heart that I need to repent of and how to maneuver in the upcoming seasons. He tells me what to study in His Word and instructs me to fast, sow, worship, etc. The Holy Spirit is our teacher, not us. Pride will cause someone to be their own instructor. The spirit of pride will lie and tell someone that they are flawless.

Prideful people will never apologize or try to make peace. Many people in the Body of Christ have mistreated each other. Many times, I was wrong or had an attitude with someone. The Holy Spirit dealt with me, and I had to humble myself and go apologize. Sometimes, I wasn't at fault and decided to make peace by not arguing or doing retaliatory acts by getting in my flesh. So I walked away or didn't respond. I trusted God to fight my battles because He knows how to get us to the end of ourselves. If I had taken matters into my own hands, things would have escalated in the wrong direction, and a physical altercation may have occurred. I never want to make a mistake and go back to jail for anyone. A prideful person feels like they have to get the last word. Prideful ministers have a hard time getting along with others. Humble yourself!

Pride will have a minister's ego puffed up. Many times a wounded leader may feel insecure and they thrive off of people's praises. They need the affirmations of others, and it hurts them to hear people esteeming others and not them. As a result, they may feel threatened by the one people are celebrating or being blessed by. A prideful person needs the spotlight. They have a hard time discerning what God wants to do in the atmosphere and they lose focus of the heart of God. They fail to realize that God can use anyone He desires to, and it's not about them. It's all about Jesus.

A prideful person demands respect and a pedestal. They feel like the world caters to them. If someone doesn't address them by a title, they become upset and may get an attitude. Many times, people don't know I am a prophet and don't recognize me as one. I am not bothered because I know who I am and my calling given by God. As long as I do the work, the fruit will speak for itself. I prophesy almost daily. Sometimes, I do it at will because the Holy Spirit gave me a gift to serve His people. I serve on my prayer line without a big crowd or a spotlight on me. The Lord is delivering and healing people daily right on the prayer line. However, when I meet someone for the first time, they may think I'm younger than I am. Or they may address me as an evangelist because of their theological belief that women can't be prophets or preachers. They may even call me Kimberly, and that's okay. If the Lord provides the unction for me to flow in His gifts, then I gladly follow His leading because we must be ready in and out of season. I discovered that as I stay faithful to God and my mandate, honor and respect will follow. I don't have to demand respect or a pedestal. God will place it on people's hearts to want to bless me.

Prideful people boast about their own success. We must remember it was the Lord who allowed us to be successful. Yes, we may have worked hard to achieve our goals. However, it was the Lord who protected, prospered, favored, and blessed us. God allowed the result of growth. We may have been used powerfully in a service. When God did the miraculous through us, we must remember it was the Lord using us. We aren't the healer. Jesus is. It's His signs and wonders that follow us. We aren't the source. He is. Sometimes, the Lord uses me in a way that blows my mind. I have seen the Lord do many miracles through my ministry. Sometimes, I am not even praying for a particular sickness to be healed, but someone comes to me and says, "I had a migraine all day, and as soon as you started praying, the pain left." Once, someone told me, "I was on my way to the hospital because I had this pain in my chest for days. You said someone here has chest pain and called it out. When you did that, the pain left immediately." When I get testimonies, I stop and make sure to give God praise because it's not me doing the healing. It's Jesus Christ. I also tell the people to give God glory for their breakthrough. Everything I have is because the Lord has allowed me to have it. I learned that we may have natural things, but tragedy can hit, and we can no longer have those things. For instance, divorce, fires, floods, death, etc., can cause us to lose our assets. We must look to God as our ultimate provider. Remember, *"Pride goes before destruction (Proverbs 16:18)."*

DANGERS

1. Refusing to listen to advice from others.
   * Don't be wise in your own eyes (Proverbs 3:7).
   * A prideful leader feels like they know it all, and wants you to believe they know more than they actually do.
   * They feel like they have been down a particular road, and the hurt from failed relationships will cause them to put up walls and make inner vows.
   * Even if they are wrong, they will not listen because their heart is so stony, and they will do what they want. They may feel the advice is an attack and get offended or hold grudges.
2. Refusing to admit their mistakes.
   * A prideful leader won't admit when they are wrong and shun any insinuation that the mistake was theirs.
   * When their team or congregation makes a mistake, they will refuse ownership of their team's failures and drag them into the mud. They always feel it's someone else's fault when goals aren't reached, and they don't learn from failure. We must realize that there is wisdom in the trials.
   * They don't see the log in their eye but see the speck in their brother's eyes (Matthew 7:3).

- They will never admit their weakness because they are afraid to be seen as vulnerable.
3. Protecting their position no matter what
   - Prideful leaders will stifle others' growth and limit their exposure so they can remain in power. They are controlling and don't want anyone to surpass them.
   - They will boast about all their accomplishments and ensure everyone knows it.
4. Wants all the glory.
   - This leader will take credit for everything their team has done. They want the microphone and their name on every award. They want the recognition and all the attention. They want to make sure no one steals their applauses.

SOLUTIONS

1. Listen to advice from others.
   - In the multitude of counselors, there is safety (Proverbs 11:14).
2. Admit when you are wrong because it shows a posture of humility.
   - Confess your sins to one another so you can be healed.
   - Admit weaknesses because when we are weak, God is strong (2 Corinthians 12:10).
3. Realize that promotion comes from God. When it's time to step down, then do so.
4. Give God all the glory.

DECLARATIONS

I decree that I will give God all the glory.
I decree that I will admit when I am wrong and walk in humility.

I decree that I will listen to advice from others and not be wise in my own eyes.

Lord, I release all pain, insecurity, jealousy, and envy to you Lord.

I decree that if I want to boast, I will boast in the Lord.

I bind up the works of the flesh and loose the fruits of the Holy Spirit.

I bind up witchcraft and any demonic seeds that are planted in me in Jesus' name.

I bind up the spirit of death and sabotage in Jesus' name.

CHAPTER 6

Loneliness

Have you ever been in a crowd full of people but felt alone and naked? Perhaps you felt like your imperfections would show and wanted to run and hide. Have you ever thought, "Who can I trust? Who can pray for me without judging me? I don't have any friends that I can share this with?" I've been there and thought these very same questions.

Many people feel like this due to loneliness and being hurt from trial after trial. So many ministry leaders have been hurt, and it caused them to enter a place of isolation that resulted in loneliness. Over time, they developed trust issues and didn't have many friends. Instead of working with others to complete a particular assignment, they found out they had to do it alone. Because of extreme hurt, they decided to keep to themselves and not fellowship with others. Most leaders don't choose to be antisocial, but they struggle with connecting with others due to many failed relationships.

I have been let down many times, and it caused me to be more reserved. It's like I had this invisible wall and didn't want to make new connections or friends. I didn't want to waste time fellowshipping with others, so I didn't attend church functions or invitations due to the scars on my heart. How can one make new friends if they don't show themselves friendly?

Proverbs 18:24 says, "A man that hath friends must shew himself friendly: and there is a friend that sticketh closer than a brother."

God had to show me that I was overly critical and that I had already predetermined that any new relationship I would make would fail. Not everyone is out to cause you harm, and not everyone is out to get you.

Loneliness can cause you to falsely judge those God sent in your life to be a blessing. We should never judge from a place of hurt, but we need to judge by the Spirit of God. In other words, we need to stop looking at things from a natural perspective or from our flesh.

1 Corinthians 2:15 says, "But he that is spiritual judgeth all things, yet he himself is judged of no man."

Once, I came under an attack from the spirit of desertion. Everyone who used to be a part of my team left because an individual convinced the people to follow after them. I remember it like yesterday, and I didn't understand what I had done. I started to recall the warnings I received about this particular individual years in advance and the uneasy feeling that always sat in my stomach each time I interacted with them. Over time, I dismissed the feelings, but how I felt proved true. They had an agenda, but I decided not to let my heart grow bitter.

When I started in ministry, it was just me. I didn't have a team, but as I obeyed God, He added to my ministry. I realized that God built my ministry and will do it again. Unless the Lord builds the house, those that labor, labor in vain (Psalm 127:1). I'm just a steward over this ministry He gave unto me, and if the Holy Ghost checks my spirit about someone, then I best take heed. So after I came underneath that attack, I had to learn how to readjust. The people I used to call on were no longer there. They exposed what was in their hearts, and that's okay. I choose to bless and forgive them. I drew closer to the Lord so He could send replacements. He called me to ministry. I didn't call myself. Preaching was the last thing I thought I would ever do, so it is the Lord's responsibility to see my ministry grow and flourish. He will bring the increase and finish what He started.

Sometimes, I didn't want to mentor anyone; I just wanted to be alone. I wanted to go into a spiritual cave, cut my phone off, and disappear. But that's not healthy, and I desperately needed deliverance; the source of my feeling or the urge to shrink back was due to fear. I feared opening up myself again or being vulnerable because I didn't want to be hurt or let down. I felt no one appreciated my ministry or the service I poured out daily. My peers misunderstood me, so I had to withdraw myself from the scene to seek the Lord for deliverance. Now, I can testify that I'm not alone because God will never leave or forsake me. His presence is ever so strong in my life, and He makes Himself so tangible.

Going through an isolation season or period of loneliness was necessary so I could be better equipped to do what God has ahead. The Lord showed me how my thoughts were all wrong. I felt pressured to quit, even though I had help. My mind thought I didn't have true support. I should have realized people were busy, and they weren't avoiding me. We will go through different phases of ministry and even warfare, but we must not let that stop us. Our Lord and Savior faced loneliness when everyone left Him. The disciples scattered, but He overcame it and fulfilled what He was called to do.

CHAPTER 6 LONELINESS

Matthew 26:56 says, "But all this was done, that the scriptures of the prophets might be fulfilled. Then all the disciples forsook him, and fled."

Jesus is our example to follow on this earth, and we can overcome loneliness, too. Stop reliving the pain and let it go. Keep your peace, and the Lord will fight for you *(Exodus 14:14)*.

DANGERS

1. Feeling like you can't talk to anyone. Bottling up the pain can lead to quitting ministry or suicide.
2. Feeling like they need to hide their private struggle to protect their public image
3. Shutting down and even shutting God out.
4. Reliving the hurt and not being open to new relationships

SOLUTIONS

1. Confess your sins to one another so you can be healed (James 5:16). Believe God for a trustworthy friend who can pray for you.
2. Don't feel pressured to be perfect: People have put too much pressure on church leaders and expect them to be perfect. Looking through the Bible, most of God's chosen people had problems but were anointed and loved God: Moses (who killed a man), David (who committed adultery), and Solomon (who served other gods).
3. Find a friend in Jesus if you are feeling lonely.
4. Be open to new connections as God restores your life.

DECLARATIONS

I bind up the spirit of loneliness in Jesus' name.

I will not re-live hurt and despair in Jesus' name.

I will let go and trust God to vindicate and restore me.

I will show myself friendly and not operate out of a place of pain.

I will bless and pray for those who left or disappointed me.

I will believe God to send me godly connections and friends whom I can trust.

I decree that the Lord is with me always, and He will never leave me.

I won't shrink back or quit my ministry assignment.

I decree that God will restore my life and send the right people to undergird me.

I am delivered, whole, and free from the spirit of loneliness in Jesus' name.

CHAPTER 7

Betrayal

Psalm 41:9 says, "Even my closest friend whom I trusted, the one who ate my bread, has lifted his heel against me."

Psalm 55:12-14 says, "For it is not an enemy who insults me— I could have handled that— nor is it someone who hates me and who now arises against me— I could have hidden myself from him— but it is you— a man whom I treated as my equal— my personal confidant, my close friend! We had good fellowship together; and we even walked together in the house of God!"

Job 19:19 says, "My close friends detest me. Those I loved have turned against me."

We all will go through betrayal in life and ministry. Jesus was in leadership, and He faced betrayal by one of his disciples, Judas. He poured into Judas daily. He taught him, and they traveled and ate together. Yet when an opportunity arose for Judas to get money, he turned on Jesus (Matthew 26:15). Ouch. I learned in ministry that people come and go. Some may feel like they have outgrown you. Others may begin to despise you. People will walk away. Whatever the circumstances, we must be okay with it and let it go. It's painful, but God will get us through. According to the Oxford Dictionary, betrayal can mean exposing one to danger by treacherously giving information to an enemy. It can also mean breaking one's promises, being disloyal to, unfaithful, or breaking faith with. Do any of these definitions sound familiar?

I can recall a time when my late pastor told me a story. He said his assistant pastor went behind his back and held a meeting. The purpose of the meeting was to get him fired and for the assistant pastor to take his place. The meeting didn't go as planned because not everyone agreed with the assistant pastor. As a result, someone told my late pastor about the secret meeting, and he soon discovered who was not really for him. My late pastor was devastated because his right-hand man undermined him and tried to steal everything he labored for over many years. The church ended up splitting, which caused more hurt. My late pastor still had to function and preach the Sunday and Wednesday services. He used to cry himself to sleep and battled discouragement until he got healing from the Lord. When my late pastor told me this story, I didn't realize I would face the same thing many years later.

One day, my husband and I talked, and he said, "Babe, it's crazy how some leave your ministry as an enemy." I said, "Yeah, it truly is. I know in my heart I never did anything to those people, but I guess it comes with the calling." He told me he reached out to this lady to thank her for sticking with me throughout the years. He said out of all the women who left my ministry, the lady who he reached out to didn't leave and was mature enough to discern the motive of the person operating in an Absalom spirit against me. Therefore she didn't follow the crowd but she obeyed God and stayed connected to my ministry.

I have found comfort in John 15:18 that if the world hated Jesus, then they would hate me also. My job is to love people because that's what God commands us to do. I can't focus on how people feel about me, but I need to focus on the Lord to have perfect peace and not get distracted from my assignment.

One day, I felt the urge to reach out to two sisters. I knew something was wrong because one sister looked at the message and never responded. The other sister responded many days later after viewing my message. Her response mentioned that she would no longer join my prayer ministry. I told her, "That's okay. I love you and am here for you if you ever need me." I just blessed them and brushed it off. Well, months went by, and the sister who did respond called me crying. She was sick unto death and said she could feel her soul leaving her body. She began to apologize and told me that her sister was spreading lies about me, saying "Prophetess K prays against you, and she is very mad at you." I asked the lady, "Why would I do that? And why would I be mad at you? I take my prayer ministry very seriously and never pray against anyone." The lady said she realized that her sister was operating underneath some Jezebel spirit and repented for believing lies about me. I told the lady that it was water underneath the bridge, and I prayed for her to live and not die to declare the works of the Lord. The lady recovered and lived as God intervened on her behalf.

When I discovered everything the other sister said about me, I wasn't surprised because I felt it in the spirit, and her never responding to me was further evidence that there was a problem. I later found out that this lady was following a false prophet who is known as a hectic in the Body of Christ. I believe his teaching influenced her mindset and allowed the enemy to mess with her thoughts. I knew it was the devil behind everything. He has been planting seeds in people's minds and hearts for years against their leaders. Again, look at Judas and Jesus' example. This person was someone who I cast the devil out of and prayed the devil off on many occasions. I promoted and vouched for them as a character witness. Yet, somehow, this individual allowed the devil to come and plant a seed. This was a betrayal; it took God to touch my heart, not to be bitter but to love many. I felt sorry for this person because they are lost and needed deliverance. Many leaders shut down and don't want to continue in their call when they face betrayal. We can overcome this by recognizing the devil behind the person.

Years ago, I was an armor bearer to the First Lady and on the intercession team of a particular ministry. I was going through a divorce that I didn't want, and my ex-husband at the time kept trying to come around and sleep with me. Since we were still married, I didn't deny him, but I was hurt because he didn't want me as a wife but only wanted sex. Well, I told the first lady what was occurring. She went and told this lady who I prayed with on the intercession team, "I'm sick of Kimberly." Then she proceeded to repeat to her everything that I confided in her. It got back to me. I was hurt because I looked up to the First Lady, and didn't know what to do. I continued to attend that church for another month until the church split into threes. The First Lady had a problem with gossiping and during one revival night, a guest speaker had the fire of God burning strongly through her. She laid hands on the First Lady, and she purged for a long time in front of the church as she received deliverance. A week or two later, the church split happened. I did not attend church for an entire year because I was wounded. I did listen to preaching throughout the day on Periscope and YouTube. I also ministered and served others with the spiritual gifts the Lord gave me. Then one day, the Lord spoke and instructed me to get back in church, and I obeyed.

Years later, there was this lady who invited me to speak at her event. It was during my wedding anniversary, and I decided to do it just to help her out.

My husband allowed me to do it because we didn't have much money to do much at that time and he knew that I would receive a love offering to help cover some of our living expenses. Over time the lady and I would message each other on social media maybe twice a year to say hello. Well years went by and she sent my husband a message saying she had a problem with me. When he told me, I was shocked. I couldn't understand what occurred that would cause this riff so I reached out to her to find out what happened. I apologized to her if I did or said anything to cause her to become upset with me. I knew in my heart I never did anything to offend her. I never talked behind her back or ignored her so I was totally lost about her response. I believe she was mad because I stopped liking her posts. To this day, I am still not sure. She ultimately said the devil was playing with her mind and since I reached out the offense has been lifted. Well, everything she said was a lie. Months went by and I thought we were cool but she ended up unfriending me on social media. I realize that people will change in their feelings towards you on a whim. Some people will not like you regardless of what you do. No matter how nice you try to treat them, it won't matter when their minds have changed. I knew it was the enemy messing with her, so I blessed her and kept it moving.

Now there were times when I was in the wrong in the way I handled others, and the Holy Spirit convicted me. I had to humble myself and apologize to the person. But in these cases, it was nothing except the devil causing confusion and planting seeds of offense, hurt, and hatred. Whenever there is envy and strife, there will be every evil work (James 3:16).

Isaiah 53:3 says, "He (Christ) was despised and rejected by men, a man of sorrows, and familiar with suffering." We are not alone in our pain. One of the sorrows Jesus experienced was the sorrow of betrayal. Judas, one of His closest teammates, eventually betrayed Him with a kiss. This was a man who had been a close companion of Jesus for over three years. He had ministered with Jesus.

What did Christ do when Judas betrayed Him? In Matthew 26:50, He called him "friend." In the very act of betrayal Jesus called His betrayer "friend." Even though Jesus' heart hurt, there was no time for bitterness, hate, or retaliation. There was Kingdom work still to be done. In the midst of betrayal, Jesus had to get on with it. Stop blaming yourself for people's actions. I used to cry and search inwardly about why people turned on me. I couldn't find any reasons and it gave me peace to continue to do what God called me to do.

DANGERS

1. Many leaders are afraid to confront others when they are out of line and presenting offensive behaviors or acting in a way that is unbecoming as a child of God. Don't overreact when you get hurt by getting in your flesh or preaching hate and hurt in your sermons. Be swift to hear, slow to speak, and slow to wrath (James 1:19).
2. Pray for wisdom and guidance in the midst of the betrayal. The Lord will show you how to handle a crisis.
3. Don't make accusations without gathering all the facts and verifying everything.
4. Don't stop communicating with someone who betrayed you because it can lead to unresolved issues.

SOLUTION

1. Leaders, please address disloyalty or any issues that arise from the beginning. Not dealing with it is like allowing cancer to spread. It will contaminate everything in its path.

2. As bad as the betrayal feels, go to the Lord in prayer. If you need to step back to heal, do so because your mental health matters. Keep your emotions in check.

3. Gather the facts and verify everything, such as the exact offense, then set a boundary in place. This person is no longer considered trustworthy, so they can't be in your leadership position or your staff until they get some deliverance.

4. Communication is critical to defining the wrong doing, outlining expectations, and establishing boundaries. It can also bring healing or reconciliation and allow you to release the offense and forgive.

DECLARATIONS

I declare that I will let all betrayal and hurt go in Jesus' name.

I will not allow others' actions to cause me to stumble in my walk with God in the name of Jesus.

I declare that I will keep my heart pure and love people where they are in Jesus' name.

I will not retaliate but have a forgiving spirit in the name of Jesus.

God will strengthen me during times of betrayal.

I will not dwell on the betrayal, but I will keep my mind on Jesus to heal and go forward.

I will lean on Jesus to help me overcome any hurt and betrayal in Jesus' name.

CHAPTER 8

Rejection

Rejection doesn't feel good. Deep down, we all want to be liked by others and accepted. However, that is not always the case. For years, I didn't fit in. In school, I was not in the popular crowd. I wasn't always the first choice when being picked to be on someone's team during a game or school competition. It seemed as if nothing I ever did was good enough. I submitted books to major stores, and they turned me away. Nothing I ever did seemed to work. Time after time, I was also passed over, leaving a scar on my heart that only the Lord could heal.

One day, the Lord began to work on my mind and change my perspective. Rejection can allow one to improve their skill set and self-development. Rejection can also be God's way of protecting you from the wrong crowd, connections, doors, and seasons. No matter the rejection we face, we are accepted by God. Our Lord and Savior Jesus faced a life of rejection, but He didn't allow that to stop Him from fulfilling His assignment on Earth, and we shouldn't either.

Psalms 118:22 says, "The stone that the builders rejected has become the cornerstone."

Jesus is the chief cornerstone or the strongest point in the building, holding everything together. Without Him, everything will fall apart. People may not have valued His ministry, but it was necessary. The same concept applies to us. What God has given to those in leadership is so vital and needed in this season. However, when a leader is wounded, they allow the spirit of rejection to take deep root in their hearts instead of allowing God to heal them by spending time in His presence.

Many leaders are wounded because, initially, they weren't the people's choice. Listen, you have to encourage yourself by this very fact. Saul wasn't God's choice but the people's choice. However, David was God's choice. It's better to be a God-pleaser than a people-pleaser. Know that people may not have chosen you and refuse to support your ministry, but there's a remnant assigned to your voice, and God will allow the right people to come that will receive you for who you are in God. If I could put a quarter in a jar for how many times people have rejected me, I would literally run out of jars. Someone out there will be assigned to your life, purpose, and destiny.

Some leaders are wounded by rejection because they are never called upon or invited to speak at ministry events. I remember God called me into the ministry in 2014, and I sat for two years before I had my first ministry invite. Some would have quit, but I knew that I wasn't ready to go forth fully because I had some areas that I needed to get deliverance in, such as anxiety, pride, selfishness, lust, dishonor, etc. Over the years, the speaking invites came as God saw fit and as I waited. OPPORTUNITIES FOUND ME when I stopped focusing on who wasn't inviting me and got busy with God. Please know that every assignment isn't for everyone, and when God tells you no about a particular engagement, it's for the best. He sees the end from the beginning, and He doesn't want us getting contaminated by being yoked up with the wrong connections.

Some leaders are rejected and must need approval from others. Not everyone will be in your amen corner or clap and cheer you on. Not everyone will celebrate you. Being an author of over 48 books, the applauses grew less each time as I released another book. Not everyone was happy when God allowed me to do events in my community. I used to get discouraged because not everyone liked my social media posts or watched my videos. Then I encouraged myself, "Who am I doing this content for? Is it for God or is it for the people? I'm building for God." When that's my mindset, it doesn't matter who approves of what I am doing. God will draw whoever needs the ministry He gave to me. Just because you don't have many likes or support on something doesn't mean it's not anointed or valuable. Whatever you do, make sure it's for the glory of God.

1 Corinthians 10:31 says, "...or whatsoever ye do, do all to the glory of God."

Some leaders are rejected because of their looks or the way they minister, which determine whether they are accepted or not. Some denominations don't believe in women preachers. Others won't receive from a Black one. Some don't want to hear anything from someone younger than them. We must realize that God chooses who He wills and we aren't God. If it were up to the people in the biblical days, David would have never become the King of Israel because, to people, he was just a little shepherd's boy. We can't judge the package that God uses.

One day, a pastor told a story of how he was burned out in ministry. He is a tall, heavy-set black man, but God led him to a short white woman to restore him. Her ministry and the anointing on her life was everything that he needed to continue in his calling. He probably would not be teaching today if he rejected whom God had sent.

I remember going to a conference as a guest speaker. I have always looked at least 20 years younger, so everyone thought I was in my early twenties and felt like I was a novice. They didn't know that I had been walking with the Lord for several decades, so they had already counted me out. Some people didn't attend the service and others were shocked when they saw the anointing flow and people were slain in the Spirit, healed and delivered. After service, a gentleman approached me and said, "I owe you an apology." I said, "What for?" He said, "I misjudged you. Wow. I learned a lesson to never judge a book by its cover. Your ministry really blessed me today." God will put an anointing on your life that no one can refute. He will back you up regardless if people reject you.

Another time, I was dealing with rejection because my tongues (gift of tongues) didn't sound like everyone else's when I prayed. I would always sing in tongues instead of praying and was afraid to pray this way in public. The Lord moved me out of my comfort zone by leading me to host a daily prayer call where we only pray in tongues for one hour. Over time I embraced how I sounded. I didn't flow like many preachers either. Sometimes in the middle of preaching, I will stop and then give a word of knowledge, pray, or prophesy. Many people told me that I was unique. I believe they told me that as a nicety because they didn't want to hurt my feelings.

Once, it got back to me that a preacher, a guest speaker at a conference where I was preaching, said I wasn't a good speaker. We have two different speaking styles. She is a hooper and holler but I'm not. Just because someone is not screaming or preaching hard doesn't mean they're not anointed. Just because someone has a different worship music preference doesn't mean that they're not anointed. Many preachers will preach the Word first, then flow by praying, prophesying, etc. at the end. However, I just accepted the way God has given me His gifts, so I flow with His Spirit.

Many preachers are wounded because they try to accommodate everyone. No matter if you do your best and obey what God is calling you to do, there will always be those who are critical. They will automatically reject your efforts. Each month I put out a monthly publication called "Rejoice Essential Magazine." It's hard work because we have to write articles, place ads, gather content, edit it, then publish it. One day someone went on my social media page and typed something like, "Hey, thumbs down. Your magazine sucks." I didn't allow their negative comments to shake me. I know God gave me this magazine, so I just deleted the comment and continued to put out another magazine the next month. People have told me throughout the years that the magazine blesses them. You or your ministry may not be for everyone, but you are for someone.

A lot of leaders are wounded by rejection because someone left their ministry or church because they felt like they weren't getting fed. One of the greatest lessons I learned in ministry is that some people come and go. Bless those who want to leave and continue to do what you are called to do. Don't allow rejection to set in. Maybe you fulfilled your assignment in that person's life, and that's totally okay. There are so many more people who you are destined to help equip. God will send you people that you can pour into who will put a demand on the gifts of the Holy Spirit in your life. Yes, it hurts when someone you care for leaves. Grieve but not for too long. Get up and go pour out on the ones who are still around. The people who left didn't call you into ministry, but God did. Some of those people weren't with you when you started, and they won't be with you when you end. Stay focused on Jesus. Not everyone will like or support you. Our Lord understands this, all too well, because the very people He healed and cast demons out of, turned on Him in the end. Yet, He still fulfilled the prophecy, and you will fulfill your assignment too.

DANGERS

1. Allowing the rejection of your preaching style, advice, and leadership to halt you from your assignment.
2. Trying to be like others to get the validation of men and thinking that others are better than you.
3. Trying to be controlling when giving advice and forcing relationships to happen and doors to open.

SOLUTIONS

1. Keep leading and expect pushback when people reject your style of ministry.
2. Remember, you are unique and must stay true to who God called you to be. Everyone may not support what you do, but God will send you whom you need.
   - As God's servant, your job is to teach, rebuke, correct, and train in righteousness (2 Timothy 3:16). Not everyone will value what you bring but make sure your heart is pure.

DECLARATIONS

Lord, I break the spirit of rejection off my life and ministry in Jesus' name. Lord, I bind up the spirit of heaviness and discouragement that is associated with rejection in Jesus' name.
Lord, I thank you that I am accepted and loved by you.
Lord, restore everything that the enemy has stolen from me through the experience of rejection.

Lord, bless me to know my identity in You and be confident in what You have called me to do.

Lord, I bind up any torment and cycles of rejection in Jesus' name.

Lord, I bind up any curse of rejection that is running in my family and ministry in Jesus' name.

CHAPTER 9

Dishonor

1 Thessalonians 5:12-13 (ESV)

12 We ask you, brothers, to respect those who labor among you and are over you in the Lord and admonish you, 13 and to esteem them very highly in love because of their work. Be at peace among yourselves.

Dishonor means to bring shame or disgrace upon someone. We hear so much about honor in the Bible, such as honoring God, your parents, and each other, but many don't obey. This generation is full of dishonor. People don't reverence God, and children are constantly disrespecting their parents. Social media has provided ample space and opportunity to bash whomever users choose. So many leaders have experienced dishonor, and they are hurting from it. Moses prayed to die because the Israelites were working his nerves and dishonored him countless times (Numbers 11:15). Imagine how much pressure leaders are facing, and then the attacks from the people just add another reason for them to give up or commit suicide. The following acts are forms of dishonor that many ministry leaders have experienced.

Some ministry leaders have experienced their members coming to them for advice, but then the person fails to obey God's word. The leader then feels like they wasted their oil or cast their pearls before the swine (Matthew 7:6). Some leaders have pulled back from being as accessible and appointed counselors or other qualified people to give counsel for this very reason.

Sometimes leaders have been cursed out or even physically harmed. Some people will interrupt the middle of service, yell at the pastor, get an attitude, rebel against the church, mock the people of God, or complain about what's wrong in the church, etc. As a result, many leaders are quitting their call, keeping a distance from the people of God and some even have security around them as a protective measure.

Oftentimes, people will do videos, podcasts, blogs, etc., speaking evil of their leader or other men and women of God. People have lost the fear of the Lord and don't regard the judgment of God (Psalms 105:15). This is very dangerous. God opened up the Earth and swallowed Moses' enemies when they came against him (Numbers 16:32). He also struck Miriam with leprosy when she talked about him (Numbers 12). Some people will come against a leader, not realizing that they are God's appointed man or woman.

Some people get upset about pastor appreciation days, expect the pastor to work a full-time job, and still deliver a powerful message each week. The pastor never gets a day of rest or a vacation. When it's time to bless the pastor with a little extra, some people refuse because they think all the church wants is their money. They don't realize that after the church bills are paid, what's left for the pastor to live off of? It may not be much at all. My late pastor in Colorado only received a $400 monthly stipend or salary from the church, and his wife worked a full-time job to support their family. When the people found out how much the pastor made, we all felt guilty and started to put money in his hands to bless him because he worked so hard. He ministered at a prison once a week, fed the homeless on Tuesdays, hosted Bible studies on Wednesdays, hosted Worship Nights on Fridays, and then had Sunday services. In between these times, he poured time into the congregation by counseling them if they needed advice, attending weddings, funerals, hospital visits, etc. People don't realize how many pastors are burning out because they are overworked, underpaid, and underappreciated.

Once, I wanted to quit doing my ministry, and it was on my mind heavily for at least three months to do so. Around this time, I hosted a conference, and all of my mentees surprised me at the end. They blessed me with scented candles because they knew I loved them. Then they gathered around me, cried, and spoke about how much of a blessing I was to them. I was over-encouraged, and from that moment on, I resisted the urge to quit because people needed what God gave me to share.

Be careful how you treat your leader because they keep watch over your soul. Let's look at Hebrews 13:17 in different translations.

Hebrews 13:17 The Message (MSG)

Be responsive to your pastoral leaders. Listen to their counsel. They are alert to the condition of your lives and work under the strict supervision of God. Contribute to the joy of their leadership, not its drudgery. Why would you want to make things harder for them?

Hebrews 13:17 (NASB 1995)

Obey your leaders and submit to them, for they keep watch over your souls as those who will give an account. Let them do this with joy and not with grief, for this would be unprofitable for you.

Hebrews 13:17 New Living Translation (NLT)

Obey your spiritual leaders, and do what they say. Their work is to watch over your souls, and they are accountable to God. Give them reason to do this with joy and not with sorrow. That would certainly not be for your benefit.

Do you want your leader to quit and close down the doors of the church or their ministry? Many will answer no, but their actions have caused their leader to walk away. When a leader falls, usually the entire congregation or members scatter. For example, when David beheaded Goliath, the Philistines scattered because their leader was dead (1 Samuel 17:51). When a pastor steps down, some people may stop attending church. In contrast, others may embrace the new pastor and stay. Some people will get mad at God or get angry at other believers. So, for our benefit, we want our leaders to be blessed and happy. We want them to be mentally sound to spend more time with God and intercede for us. We need them to be encouraged and focused so they can study the Word and give us God's revelation. We want them to constantly pursue God and get saturated in His oil so they can pour into us. Remember, the anointing flows down from the beard to the skirt. We need to be able to receive; whatever we dishonor we can't receive from. Some people couldn't receive from Jesus when He went to His hometown because of dishonor (Matthew 13).

DANGERS

1. Dishonor can destroy a person and their ministry.
2. Dishonor can result in the judgment of God coming upon you.
3. Dishonor can stop you from receiving.
4. Dishonor can hinder your spiritual walk.
5. Dishonor can come back into your life.

SOLUTIONS

1. Instead of trying to bring shame, pray for them. Honor everyone in their respectful places.
2. Treat people with kindness, and don't expose your leader's sins even if you know of your leader's sins. When Noah got drunk in Genesis 9, his son Ham saw his father's nakedness and exposed him. As a result, he was cursed forever.
3. Don't expect to receive blessings from the vessel that you dishonored. The flow of oil will stop because God will not violate His principles. Honor what you want to partake in.
4. People who have brought shame to their leaders will reap it because God is not mocked. Whatever someone sows, they will reap (Galatians 6:7-8). Just pray for your leader.

DECLARATIONS

Lord, I will honor my leader's vision and their work.

Lord, I will still submit myself under leadership even if I am a leader.

Lord, bless me never to question my leader's ability or calling.

Lord, bless me never to bring shame or disgrace upon my leadership.

Lord, bless me never to expose sin in my leader's life.

Lord, bless me to never cross healthy boundaries with my leader.

Lord, bless me to never misuse my leader's name for personal gain or opportunity in Jesus' name.

CHAPTER 10

Opportunism

Imagine if people only looked at you just as an opportunity for advancement. They don't consider your feelings or needs. Their only agenda is to use you and your ministry as their launching pad, and once that happens, they are done with you. They will cut you off and no longer support or speak to you. They will no longer honor you publicly or make time for you. They never wanted a deeper relationship; maybe they were never for you. This has happened to many leaders who are hurting because of it.

The first thing we must know about opportunists is that they don't want a genuine relationship with you. They only want to use you for your platform. This is why we must not get caught up in a person's charisma or charm. We can't be blind sided from what the person is doing for us or the ministry, but we must pray about who we should promote in leadership positions or who we should have on our programs. An opportunist is very ambitious and may see a weakness in our ministry and then step up as a solution, but they are only temporary. We can't give them a permanent position because they will not stick around. God will highlight trustworthy individuals who are planted in your ministry.

The second thing we must know about opportunists is that they only want to connect to you because of who you are connected to. They look at you as a door to connect with those you know. You or your ministry isn't the goal or what they want; they want to connect with your spiritual leader, parents, influential people, etc. They will use flattery and all kinds of tactics to try to impress you, so you can introduce them to whoever is the real reason why they connected to you in the first place. Most leaders love hard and desire to help others walk in their callings. Still, we should always pray about who we promote in ministry. We need to ask God if it's this person's appointed time because maybe He wants to deliver that person from impure motives, and all we are doing is getting in the way when we promote them prematurely.

The third thing we must know about opportunists is that they will leave once they get what they want from you. Some leaders didn't see it coming, but if they would be honest, they ignored the red flags because they wanted to see the good in the person. Perhaps the people around the leader warned them about an individual, but the leader refused to listen. Maybe the leader felt checks in their spirit about this individual but brushed it off. We can't expect someone with a vagabond spirit to be stationary because they need deliverance. It's crucial as a leader to intercede for your members and ask the Lord if there is anything they need to get delivered from. Write what you hear down and ask God for wisdom on ministering to this person effectively. Our job as leaders is not to embarrass anyone, but we can have a corporate deliverance service so that person can be the main one getting delivered.

The fourth thing we must know about opportunists is that they are selfish, have impure motives, and are in your ministry for personal gain. As a leader, you want unity, love, and the people to support and encourage each other. Try to be Spirit-led and be fair across the board. Ask the Holy Spirit how you should structure your ministry, such as the departments and organizations within (children, outreach, media, prison, administrative, prayer, cell groups, singles, teens, music, etc.). Before you promote anyone, that person needs to be proven. Have they been around for a while? Were they with you during the storm? How is their character? How do they treat their family? What do others say about them in the community? What did God say about their heart? Don't expect an opportunist to be a team player. In these types of environments, they may expose themselves. Have a listening ear and a discerning spirit.

One day, I was listening to Apostle Ryan Lestrange speaking on leadership. He talked about how God expanded his ministry and took him worldwide. He then said something that stood out to me: "People will start looking at you as an opportunity. They don't want genuine relationships." When God increased his social media following, he started to deal with people connecting to him for all the wrong reasons. They saw him on TV, radio, and other major platforms and wanted him to connect them to the people who helped make it possible. They weren't connecting to serve the ministry or because the ministry blessed them. Once some of these people got on his social media platforms, they cut him off, and some even talked bad about him. He got hurt, but God helped restore him and continued to expand his ministry influence.

Another time, I was scrolling on Facebook, and this young man openly repented. He said that he moved to a city near this prophet with a huge social media following. He went to her ministry and tried so hard to connect, to get promoted to speak, and to get his gifts used there, but it never happened. He became so frustrated and even grew bitter and left her ministry. He sought God, and the Lord revealed to him that his reasons for going there were wrong and he was seeking man, not God. That's why God blocked the promotion because he loved this man so much that he knew that what he wanted was not in God's perfect timing for his life. There was so much refining to do. The man confessed that God never told him to move and warned people about being an opportunist. I admire and respect this young man for his courage to repent openly.

We know about Elisha and Elijah and the double portion anointing. When God took Elijah up to heaven, Elisha got a double portion of Elijah's spirit after serving him for many years (2 Kings 2). However, Gehazi, Elisha's mentee, never received the double portion anointing. Why? Because Gehazi was an opportunist. He was greedy and wanted personal gain. In ministry, God sometimes tells us to bless people and not take a dime. Our gifts are not for purchase, and we can't be bought. If we let people pay us to prophesy or to flow in the gifts of the spirit, then we are nothing more than diviners. Naaman was a man of great influence, but he had leprosy. It was embarrassing because people would excommunicate you, or you would have to be quarantined outside of society. So here is this powerful man, having to hide his scars from this disease. He hears about the prophet Elisha, sees him, and is told to dip down in the nasty Jordan River seven times. Naaman initially got offended but desperately wanted healing, so he obeyed. Miraculously, he was healed, and as a result, he wanted to pay Elisha, but Elisha said no. Gehazi goes behind Elisha's back and approaches Naaman. Naaman gives money and clothes to Gehazi. God revealed to Elisha what was occurring. Gehazi, being an opportunist, ended up with leprosy, and it was the end of his ministry (2 Kings 5).

Pay attention to the words people speak. One lady told me that her class was on a higher level than mine. At first, I thought nothing about it, but it didn't sit right with my husband. He told me she had no business saying that, and he was right. Why was she even comparing her classes to mine, especially when they blessed her and got her to where she was in ministry? It was competition and pride.

One day, the same lady called me to say she felt connected to my spiritual father and wanted to be underneath his ministry. She wanted to bypass me to get to him. However, he discerned her motives and refused to even connect with her. When she called, I told her that I felt like she was an opportunist, and she cried. I kept this in the back of my mind. A few months went by, and she caused division in my ministry by turning people against me. The entire time she tried to make connections with my connections. I was trained that my leader's door isn't my door, and when my leader invites me to the table with other influential people, be quiet and never try to outshine my leader. I have been at the table with TV reps and others with great platforms. Some were impressed by those who displayed humility but were turned off by those with pride who felt the need to boast about all their accomplishments. As a result, I got on TV and had a radio broadcast. I never asked for it, but it was given to me for a season. Going to dinner was just to fellowship and serve my leader. It wasn't about me trying to force myself and connect with a TV executive. I never disconnected from my leader after this great opportunity. God knows when you are ready and what you can handle.

Opportunists will serve and butter up to you, then expose themselves as they go after what they want. Nothing is wrong with wanting to advance, but it's all about motives. Their motive wasn't to serve you unto God. Their motive was to become famous, etc.

DANGERS

1. Many leaders are scared to connect with others because of what they dealt with, but God is a deliverer.

2. Many leaders are still determining who they can trust, but ask the Lord to send you trustworthy people.

3. Many leaders don't want to lead others due to the pain of being used and abused. Allow God to mend your broken heart.

SOLUTIONS

1. Pray about who to connect with and who to promote.
2. Stay loving, but be discerning in the process.
3. Resist the urge to quit. God will send an Aaron and Hur to hold up your arms and be with you on the battlefield (Exodus 17).

DECLARATIONS

Lord, I will not be an opportunist in Jesus' name.

Lord, if people have hurt me because they used and abused me, heal me from those broken relationships.

Lord, bless me to be discerning, loving, and Spirit-led.

Lord, bless me always pray about who I should promote and allow in my inner circle.

Lord, bless me to never give up on my God-given assignment because of what people have done to me.

Lord, send me trustworthy people in my ministry who have a heart to serve you.

CHAPTER 11

Forgotten

    Imagine constantly pouring out or serving a group of people and meeting their needs. However, when it comes to your fulfillment, they aren't around. Welcome to the world of pastoring. When we think of pastoring, we imagine a shepherd; when we think of church members, we see sheep. Jesus is our good shepherd. He is always looking out for us and leading and guiding us. Our job as leaders and pastors is to look out for the sheep and protect them from ravenous wolves in sheep's clothing (Matthew 7:15). Yet, the sheep aren't concerned about the shepherd's well-being. Many leaders feel forgotten by their members and sometimes God.

    Years ago, I was an armor bearer to a prophetess in my area. I was single and struggling financially. I had no idea this prophetess and her husband were also struggling. I would find out months later that they had to put their house and car up for collateral to keep their church open (paying the mortgage on that property). I had been fasting and praying, and finally, I got a financial breakthrough. I could pay my rent, put gas in my car so I could go to work, and buy some basic groceries (bread, ramen, milk, cereal, beans, and rice). When I got the money, I picked up the phone and told the prophetess what God had done. Immediately, she smacked her lips and responded, "God, what about me?" She wasn't even happy for me but only focused on her circumstances. We got off the phone and I went into prayer crying. I stayed in that ministry and continued to serve, but the prophetess never knew how much she hurt me. At that time, I was very fragile, and anything could make me cry. Over the years, I grew tougher skin. Now, I believe this prophetess felt forgotten, and her pain came out of her mouth because out of the abundance of the heart the mouth speaks (Matthew 12:34). We can't effectively lead people if we can't be happy for them and rejoice with them. We are supposed to rejoice with those who rejoice (Romans 12:15). You may be hurting, but as you spend time with the Lord, you will be able to have steadfastness and self-control. You won't blurt out what's in your heart and will be encouraged if God has blessed those around you because that indicates that you are NEXT!

Many times, I didn't have a Christmas, birthday, or Thanksgiving because I was broke. I felt like a horrible mom because I couldn't get my children any gifts. I didn't go out to dinner because I couldn't afford it. I didn't cook a holiday feast because it was just too expensive. The people in my ministry who sit underneath my teachings, weekly prayers, and broadcasts weren't sowing. When I asked them to support the ministry, very few gave. These people received prophecy, deliverance, healing, encouragement, etc. I don't charge for these things, but if we preach the Gospel, we should live by the Gospel. 1 Corinthians 9:14 says, "In the same way, the Lord commanded that those who proclaim the gospel should get their living by the gospel."

Why muzzle the ox that treads the corn (Duet. 25:4)? Do not muzzle an ox while it is working to produce grain. The ox (pastor, leader, trailblazer) deserves to partake in some of his own labor. I felt forgotten by the people. Many people are sitting in a ministry where they are fed but will give to another ministry when their favorite speaker comes to town. This hurts many leaders and they grew bitter.

When no one gave to me during the most critical times, such as hosting a conference or wanting to expand my media ministry, I had to encourage myself. I didn't slack up in my preaching or serving, but I went to God and spent more time with Him. As a result, He blessed me. He sent random people who came across my ministry on YouTube or social media to sow a significant seed. He assigned people to my ministry who would sustain me just like Elijah being supported by the ravens with bread and the widow at Zarephath (1 Kings 17).

When I blessed the people without looking for anything in return, God would, in return, bless me from an unlikely source. We can't tell God how to bless us or who to use to bless us. Over the years, things did get dry during certain seasons, but God is so faithful to provide.

I have always been an entrepreneur. At the age of 12, I learned how to braid my own hair. I got so good at it I started braiding everyone's hair in the neighborhood and even some of my teachers' hair. At 16, I bought my first car from braiding hair. Even though the car was a lemon, God put that drive inside of me to make money by setting my own schedule. He knew that one day, He would call me to preach His Word and didn't want me to be restricted by a typical 8-hours job with only 1 week of vacation time a year and no weekends off.

God allowed me to go to school and get certificates in Phlebotomy and Chiropractic assistant. He allowed me to get an Associate's Degree in Respiratory Therapy and a Bachelor's in Biology and Chemistry. As I was working to get my Master's in Public Health, God intervened and called me to preach His Word. He told me to stop trying to attend medical school because school was an idol in my life. He allowed me to continue to work as a Respiratory Therapist for a few more years, and then it was time for me to transition into full-time ministry: living by faith and trusting God to send the money to pay my bills and do ministry work.

It was trying at times, but I sought God for a strategy to have income. He allowed me to write books and gave me a publishing company. I didn't even know that I had that in me to do, but God can pull out the best gifts and talents on the inside. Having a business allowed me to do ministry without motives. Some preachers only get on social media to get money, and they will use manipulative tactics to get people to sow. We have to trust God to provide. Certain seasons have been better than the others, but when I asked the Lord to allow me to have 7 income streams, the wells started to dry up again. Sometimes, we don't move if we are comfortable. We move when we get uncomfortable. Elijah didn't move until the brook dried up. He had bread and food, so he was good until the water ran out (1 Kings 17).

Things started to dry up in 2022, and I felt forgotten about by everyone. God led me to an insurance job and I became a licensed insurance agent in many states. Receiving this source of income was a blessing because I could now do things for my family and have a vacation. After all, I was on the verge of burning out. The last vacation I had was in 2007 or 2008. So, in 2022, I was desperately in need of one.

In Deuteronomy 18, the Levites inherited the Lord and had to live on food offerings presented to the Lord. While the other tribes received land, the Levites received none. However, certain cities were given to them to do God's work. They were to set up tabernacles and serve in the Lord's house. In Numbers 18, the Levites were given tithes in return for their work while serving in the Tabernacle. The Lord gave the Levites a vocation and provided them with sustenance. He is doing the same for His leaders.

Just because the people forgot about you doesn't mean God forgot. You will be well off. God is looking at how you respond in dry seasons and seeing if you will trust Him. Don't ever think that God has forgotten you when things aren't happening as fast as you desire. I had to encourage myself many times with these verses and you should do the same.

Hebrews 13:5–6 (ESV) says, "Keep your life free from love of money, and be content with what you have, for he has said, "I will never leave you nor forsake you." 6 So we can confidently say, "The Lord is my helper; I will not fear; what can man do to me?"

Everything will happen in God's timing. I will have great birthday celebrations, holidays, and I will be able to provide for my family and take that much needed vacation. While I'm waiting, I am going to be patient and rejoice.

James 1:4 says, "But let patience have her perfect work, that ye may be perfect and entire, wanting nothing."

1 Thessalonians 5:16-17 says, "Rejoice always, pray without ceasing, give thanks in all circumstances; for this is the will of God in Christ Jesus for you."

DANGERS

1. Thinking the wrong thoughts.
2. Getting discouraged and bitter because the people aren't supporting you as you desire.
3. Giving up on your God assignment because you don't see the fruit of your labor.

SOLUTIONS

1. We must renew our minds and constantly encourage ourselves that things will turn around.
2. We must keep our hearts pure and never mistreat God's people. They aren't our source; God is our source. He will provide all that we need.
3. We must be faithful to the end. T.D. Jakes had a small storefront ministry for about 12 years before the late Paul Crouch discovered him. He had holes in his clothes and many times his family went without, but look at what the Lord has done. God is no respecter of a person (Acts 10:34). If He does it for one, He can do it for all.

DECLARATIONS

Lord, bless me never to quit but to keep pressing even when things get tough.

Lord, thank you for never leaving nor forsaking me.

Lord, thanks for sending people to sustain and bless my ministry.

Lord, thanks for sending all the resources that I need to fulfill my assignment.

Lord, bless me to have the right attitude as I wait on your promises.

Lord, bless me to be patient and never get ahead of you.

I decree that I will have an attitude of gratitude in Jesus' name. Amen.

About The Author

Kimberly Moses started off her ministry as Kimberly Hargraves. She is highly sought after as a prophetic voice, intercessor and prolific author. There is no doubt that she has a global mandate on her life to serve the nations of the world by spreading the Gospel of Jesus Christ. She has a quickly expanding worldwide healing and deliverance ministry. Kimberly Moses wears many hats to fulfill the call God has placed on her life as an entrepreneur over several businesses including her own personal brand Rejoice Essentials which promotes the Gospel of Jesus Christ.

She also serves as a life coach and mentor to many women. She is also the loving mother of two wonderful children. She is married to Tron. Kimberly has dedicated her life to the work of ministry and to serve others under the call God has placed over her life. Kimberly currently resides in South Carolina.

She is a very anointed woman of God who signs, miracles and wonders follow. The miraculous and incessant testimonies attributed to her ministry are incalculable, with many reporting physical and mental healing, financial breakthroughs, debt cancellations and other favorable outcomes. She is known across the globe as a servant who truly labors on behalf of God's people through intercession.

She is the author of The Following:

"Overcoming Difficult Life Experiences with Scriptures and Prayers"
"Overcoming Emotions with Prayers"
"Daily Prayers That Bring Changes"
"In Right Standing,"
"Obedience Is Key,"
"Prayers That Break The Yoke Of The Enemy: A Book Of Declarations,"
"Prayers That Demolish Demonic Strongholds: A Book Of Declarations,"
"Work Smarter. Not Harder. A Book Of Declarations For The Workforce,"
"Set The Captives Free: A Book Of Deliverance."
"Pray More Challenge"
"Walk By Faith: A Daily Devotional"
"Empowering The New Me: Fifty Tips To Becoming A Godly Woman"
"School of the Prophets: A Curriculum For Success"
"8 Keys To Accessing The Supernatural"
"Conquering The Mind: A Daily Devotional"
"Enhancing The Prophetic In You"
"The ABCs of The Prophetic: Prophetic Characteristics"
"Wisdom Is The Principal Thing: A Daily Devotional"
"It Cost Me Everything"
"The Making Of A Prophet: Women Walking in Prophetic Destiny"
"The Art of Meditation: A Daily Devotional"
"Warfare Strategies: Biblical Weapons"
"Becoming A Better You"
"I Almost Died"
"The Pastor's Secret: The D.L. Series"
"June Bug The Busy Bee: The Gamer"
"June Bug The Busy Bee: The Bully"
"The Weary Prophet: Providing Practical Steps For Restoration"
"The Insignificant Woman"

"The Foolish Woman: A Daily Devotional"
"June Bug The Busy Bee: Sibling Rivalry"
"All Things Relationships"
"30 Day Pray For Your Spouse Challenge"
"The Christian Drama Queen Mentality"
"30 Days Praying For The Nations"
"Intercessor's Prayer Notebook"
"Prayer Request Notebook Fervent Effectual Prayers Of The Righteous"
"The Prophet's Notebook"
"The Photographer's Assistant"
"The Ultimate Entrepreneur"
"Diabetic Caretaker Blood Sugar Log"
"The Preacher's Handbook"
"Christian Weight Loss Journal"
"Couple's Recipe Meal Planner And Notebook"
"Prophetic Dreams And Visions Journal"
"The Therapist Secret: The D.L. Series"
"Tabuletta"
"Tested, Tried, But I Survived"

You can find more about Kimberly at
www.kimberlyhargraves.com

For Rejoice Essential Magazine, visit
www.rejoiceessential.com

For beauty, hair, and t-shirts, visit
www.rejoicingbeauty.com

Please write a review for my books on Amazon.com

Support this ministry:
Cashapp: $ProphetKimberlyMoses
Paypal.me/remag
Venmo: Kimberly-Moses-19

Follow my YouTube Channels:
Kimberly Moses
Kimberly Finds

Index

flesh, 1, 16, 22, 23, 25, 28, 30, 33, 34, 35, 37, 38, 39, 40, 41, 45, 47, 56

forgive, 3, 14, 31, 48, 57

Forgotten, 4, 76

freedom, 4

funerals, 67

G

Gad, 19

Gehazi, 73

Gentiles, 24, 25

glory, 16, 19, 39, 43, 44, 60

God, 2, 3, 4, 5, 6, 7, 8, 9, 10, 11, 12, 13, 15, 16, 17, 18, 19, 20, 21, 22, 23, 25, 26, 27, 28, 30, 31, 32, 33, 34, 35, 36, 37, 38, 39, 40, 41, 42, 43, 44, 47, 48, 49, 50, 51, 52, 53, 54, 56, 57, 58, 59, 60, 61, 62, 63, 65, 66, 67, 68, 69, 71, 72, 73, 74, 75, 76, 77, 78, 79, 80, 81, 82

Goliath, 68

Gospel, 20, 24, 25, 77, 82

gossip, 7, 31

government, 14, 24

grace, 23, 32, 37

Grieve, 62

guilty, 15, 66

H

handkerchief, 26

happy, 35, 60, 68, 77

havoc, 17

healing, 2, 4, 9, 29, 30, 35, 42, 43, 52, 57, 73, 77, 82

I

J

jail, 41
jealous, 5, 20
jealousy, 16, 22, 23, 45
Jesus, 2, 3, 5, 6, 10, 13, 14, 16, 19, 22, 23, 24, 25, 26, 28, 29, 31, 33, 34, 37, 38, 41, 42, 43, 45, 49, 50, 51, 53, 54, 55, 56, 57, 58, 59, 62, 63, 64, 68, 69, 75, 76, 80, 81, 82
Jews, 24, 25
Jezebel, 53
Jim Crow laws, 27
Joe Biden, 25
Jordan River, 73
Judas, 51, 54, 55, 56

K

Kathryn Kuhlman, 28
kill, 16, 40
kindness, 8, 35, 69
King, 1, 18, 19, 25, 27, 39, 40, 60
Kingdom, 18, 56
Korah, 2

L

leaders, 1, 2, 3, 15, 19, 21, 25, 29, 30, 32, 33, 44, 46, 49, 53, 54, 56, 59, 60, 62, 65, 66, 67, 68, 69, 70, 71, 74, 75, 76, 78, 79
legacy, 1
leprosy, 66, 73
Levites, 79

R

S

shepherd, 60, 76

sick, 1, 20, 26, 37, 53, 54

sicknesses, 33

sin, 19, 32, 37, 41, 69

sins, 29, 37, 44, 49, 69

sister, 2, 16, 27, 53

skin, 20, 27, 77

slander, 7

social media, 1, 7, 11, 13, 17, 18, 19, 21, 22, 55, 60, 62, 72, 78, 79

Solomon, 49

soul, 3, 26, 35, 53, 67

sovereign, 26, 37

spirit, 5, 6, 7, 8, 9, 10, 11, 13, 14, 16, 17, 18, 19, 20, 24, 25, 30, 31, 33, 37, 41, 45, 47, 48, 49, 50, 52, 53, 57, 59, 63, 71, 72, 73

spiritual cave, 48

spiritual walk, 68

steal, 16, 52

stipend, 66

stomach, 47

strength, 3

suffer, 34

suicide, 1, 49, 65

support, 19, 20, 23, 48, 59, 60, 62, 63, 66, 70, 72, 77

supporters, 6, 9

synagogue, 6

T

T.D. Jakes, 81

teach, 29, 33, 63

teammates, 55

Y

www.ingramcontent.com/pod-product-compliance
Lightning Source LLC
Chambersburg PA
CBHW071023120626
46546CB00003B/1196